REFLEXIONES

REFLEXIONES

HISPANIC MINISTRY

Timothy Matovina and Hosffman Ospino

Paulist Press
New York / Mahwah, NJ

Cover image by HelenStock/Shutterstock.com
Cover and book design by Lynn Else

Library of Congress Cataloging-in-Publication Data
Names: Matovina, Timothy, author. | Ospino, Hosffman, author.
Title: Reflexiones : hispanic ministry / Timothy Matovina and Hosffman Ospino.
Description: New York / Mahwah, NJ : Paulist Press, [2021] | Summary: "Two preeminent Hispanic Catholic voices share their observations and insights into this growing sector of the U.S. Church."— Provided by publisher.
Identifiers: LCCN 2020043736 (print) | LCCN 2020043737 (ebook) | ISBN 9780809155484 (paperback) | ISBN 9781587689468 (ebook)
Subjects: LCSH: Church work with Hispanic Americans—Catholic Church. | Hispanic American Catholics—Religious life.
Classification: LCC BX1407.H55 M385 2021 (print) | LCC BX1407.H55 (ebook) | DDC 259.089/68073—dc23
LC record available at https://lccn.loc.gov/2020043736
LC ebook record available at https://lccn.loc.gov/2020043737

ISBN 978-0-8091-5548-4 (paperback)
ISBN 978-1-58768-946-8 (e-book)

Published by Paulist Press
997 Macarthur Boulevard
Mahwah, New Jersey 07430
www.paulistpress.com

Printed and bound in the
United States of America

Contents

CONTENTS

Preface

Latinos are transforming the Catholic Church in the United States in profound ways. They are the youngest, largest, and one of the fastest-growing groups of Catholics in the country. Catholicism remains the largest religious group in our nation precisely because of Latinos. Moreover, no reflection about the American Catholic experience in the twenty-first century could be deemed credible without properly acknowledging and engaging the presence of Latinos as well as their leadership, youthfulness, ritual and devotional traditions, hunger for faith formation, theological wisdom, evangelizing apostolic movements, prophetic advocacy for justice, and vibrant faith communities. As the U.S. Catholic bishops have acknowledged, salutary values such as respect for the dignity of each person, profound love for family life, a deep sense of community, an appreciation of life as a precious gift from God, and pervasive and authentic devotion to Mary are at the heart of Hispanic cultures and ways of being in the world.

Just as we celebrate the gifts and hopes with which Hispanics build and further strengthen the U.S. Catholic experience, we are also mindful, however, of the hardships that affect the lives of millions of our sisters and brothers in this community. As we were in the process of completing this work, the COVID-19 pandemic struck, with particularly devastating consequences for Latinx communities. In locales across the country, Latinas and Latinos disproportionately lost their jobs, and with that the ability to support their families, many of them in Mexico, Latin America, and the Caribbean. In the midst of the pandemic, and like other groups living in the margins of our society, hundreds of thousands have no choice but to take the available jobs in the healthcare and service industries while risking their racialized bodies, their lives, and their families. Many who contract the virus must confront the reality of not having health insurance, or receiving subpar care, or simply avoiding a hospital altogether because of fears of deportation. Public social safety nets are unavailable to those who lack documents, often even for the thousands of first responders and healthcare workers under Deferred Action for Childhood Arrivals (DACA) status. Given these oppressive conditions, it is not surprising that Latinos are among the segments of the population being infected and dying at a higher rate than the general populace. Within the Catholic Church, we are pained to hear of Latino parish communities that have endured scores of COVID-19 deaths, usually without the possibility of gathering at funerals to mourn and pray for the deceased and those who survive them. We are also discouraged about furloughs and dismissals of colleagues who work in Hispanic ministry positions. While the economic challenges in dioceses, parishes, and schools affect church workers of all backgrounds, the sad reality is that too often Latinos are among the first to be removed during times of crisis.

This latest episode in the suffering and struggles of Hispanics in the United States is yet another compelling reality that cries out for a gospel-inspired prophetic response. We protest the injustices affecting disproportionately the lives of our Hispanic sisters and brothers during the pandemic, and we unite our voices to those of millions who protest racial prejudice and violence against Black people and other minoritized communities in the wake of the murder of George Floyd and other African Americans. If the reflections on Hispanic ministry in this volume offer some modicum of hope and insight to struggling communities and their leaders, we will consider our mission accomplished.

Reflexiones: Hispanic Ministry examines the contours of the Hispanic presence and the significance of that presence for Catholic pastoral leaders and for the wider church and society. The volume addresses two broad topics. In part 1, we explore the significance of the long Hispanic presence in what is now the United States of

America, with particular focus on the past half century. Chapters 1 and 2 take the broadest historical perspective, respectively exploring the themes of evangelization and immigration within the history and current reality of Catholicism in the United States. The next two chapters successively assess Hispanic contributions to the Vatican II renewal of the church and the particular influence of the Encuentro process in that renewal. Chapters 5 and 6 present a summary of important realities, challenges, and opportunities vis-à-vis the Hispanic presence. Together, the chapters in part 1 of the volume underscore that Latinas and Latinos have been and continue to be a vital force of revitalization for the church and its mission to marginalized persons and the wider society. Since it is not possible to comprehensively examine all the issues and concerns of Hispanic ministry in a single volume, the second part of the book delves into particular pastoral contexts in which Latinos shape and are shaped by the life and ministries of the church: parishes, apostolic movements, catechetical programs, families, and youth. We are aware that many of Latinos' apostolic endeavors, evangelical witness, and faith-inspired struggles for justice do not occur on church grounds or even with ecclesial sponsorship. Indeed, one of the gifts of Hispanics is precisely that they live their Christian discipleship at home, at work, in their neighborhoods and communities. We address these various contexts with two primary audiences in mind: Hispanic believers who strive to incarnate their faith in the circumstances of their daily lives, *en lo cotidiano*, as well as the leaders who accompany them.

The essays in this volume were previously published. Some were originally invited as presentations. Some are excerpts of longer articles. Citations for each of the original publications are given in the accompanying list of sources found in the acknowledgments below. With the exception of changes to update the material or eliminate repetition, each of the selections appears in its original form. We have used the words *Hispanic*, *Latino/a*, and *Latinx* interchangeably to reflect the usage of these words among pastoral leaders and theologians in Hispanic Catholic communities.

The genesis of this book is our many years of friendship and collaboration on the advancement of Hispanic ministry and theological reflection in the United States. As theologians working in Catholic universities, we also wish to foster a much needed conversation that should exist among academics and pastoral leaders. Numerous Hispanic ministry leaders and Latino Catholics have enriched us with their dedication, their experiences, and their wisdom. Our desire is that these reflections illuminate and animate their joys and hopes, griefs and anxieties as we walk together along the journey of faith.

Timothy Matovina
Hosffman Ospino

Acknowledgments

The authors offer thanks to the editors of the following journals and presses for their permission to reprint previously published material, presented here in the order in which the essays appear in this volume:

1. Ospino, Hosffman. "The Joy of the Gospel in America: Landscape and Priorities for Evangelization in a Diverse Church." *Origins* 47 (July 20, 2017): 163–66.
2. Matovina, Timothy. "Our History and Heritage: The Church in the U.S." *Liguorian* 95 (January 2007): 8–12.
3. Matovina, Timothy. "Latino Contributions to Vatican II Renewal." *Origins* 42 (December 20, 2012): 465–71.
4. Ospino, Hosffman. "Called and Sent to Encuentro: A Pastoral Theological Vision for the Fifth Encuentro Process." *Origins* 44 (April 2, 2015): 705–9.
5. Matovina, Timothy. "Ten Things to Know about Hispanic Catholics." *U.S. Catholic* 78 (November 2013): 23–27.
6. Ospino, Hosffman. "Ten Ways Hispanics Are Redefining American Catholicism." *America* 217 (November 13, 2017): 18–23.
7. Ospino, Hosffman. "Building Communion in Culturally Diverse Parishes." *Catholic UPDATE*, Liguori (July 2018).
8. Matovina, Timothy. "Our Lady of Guadalupe: A Refuge for Many, a Feast for All to Celebrate." *Pastoral Liturgy* 45 (September/October 2014): 4–8.
9. Matovina, Timothy. *Ministerio Hispano: Una introducción.* Notre Dame, IN: Ave Maria Press, 2016. Chapter 3, "Movimientos apostólicos."

10. Ospino, Hosffman. "The Bible and Catechesis." In *The Word of God and Latino Catholics: The Teachings of the Road to Emmaus*, ed. Jean-Pierre Ruiz and Mario J. Paredes, 51–70. New York: American Bible Society, 2012.

11. Ospino, Hosffman. "Hispanics and Family Life in Twenty-First Century America: A Catholic Call to Action." In *Renewing Catholic Family Life and Spirituality: Experts Explore New Directions in Family Spirituality and Family Ministry*, ed. Gregory K. Popcak, 299–312. Huntington, IN: Our Sunday Visitor, 2020.

12. Ospino, Hosffman. "Hispanic Young Catholics." In *Young Adult American Catholics: Explaining Vocation in Their Own Words*, ed. Maureen Day, 210–16. Mahwah, NJ: Paulist Press, 2018.

Part One

HISPANICS IN THE U.S. CHURCH AND SOCIETY

The Joy of the Gospel in the United States*

Hosffman Ospino

Dear sisters and brothers. What a wonderful time to be Catholic in the United States of America! Please join me in praising the Lord by saying together a resounding amen: Amen! Yes, amen, we are here.

I want to thank our Catholic bishops and the organizers of this convocation for gathering us as a church to reflect about our identity and vocation.

We came together to engage in a very important exercise of "evangelical discernment" (*Evangelii Gaudium* 50), as Pope Francis reminds us. We are here responding to the invitation to reflect intentionally about what it means to be missionary disciples of Jesus Christ proclaiming the joy of the gospel in every corner of our nation.

What will Catholics one hundred years from now remember about us when they look back at the first decades of the twenty-first century? How will historians define the historical period in which you

---

* Opening keynote delineating the landscape and urgent priorities for Catholic evangelization in the United States in the twenty-first century. Delivered on July 2, 2017, at the Convocation of Catholic Leaders: The Joy of the Gospel in America, convened by the United States Conference of Catholic Bishops in Orlando, Florida.

and I live? What will be our legacy? What kind of faith communities will our children and grandchildren inherit?

These questions often haunt my imagination. Although we cannot control what historians of U.S. Catholicism will write in one hundred years, we can definitely give them the best stories, our stories and those of our communities. I believe that this is why we are here at this convocation: to set the course of what can be a new Catholic moment in the United States.

It is imperative that we have the best possible understanding of who we are as Catholics in the United States and the particular contexts in which we live and practice our faith. Allow me to walk with you, sharing a few thoughts in this regard.

The large waves of Catholic immigrants arriving mainly from Western Europe during the nineteenth century quickly eclipsed the influence of the small Catholic settlements established during colonial times that preceded the birth of our nation. Many of these early communities were Hispanic and French.

In a period of roughly 150 years, the new Catholic immigrants built more than 20,000 parishes, more than 13,000 schools, hundreds of universities, hospitals, and massive networks of social services. Such presence eventually led to a strong political, cultural, and intellectual presence in the public square.

The rapid growth of Catholicism in such a short period of time was unprecedented, actually dazzling, a true miracle considering the sociopolitical circumstances that these Catholic sisters and brothers had to face, including major bouts of anti-Catholic sentiment. Much of what identifies U.S. Catholicism today is the result of those years of growth defined by a strong Euro-American cultural heritage.

Toward the middle of the twentieth century, U.S. Catholicism had entered a relatively brief period of stability. Most European immigrants had settled, and their U.S.-born children and grandchildren were quickly embracing the "American way of life." U.S. Catholics had been engaged in a long process of soul-searching about whether they should be more Catholic or more American. Eventually most opted for a both/and solution to the dilemma.

4

Millions of U.S. Catholics became highly educated; many joined the middle and upper classes of our society. A large number of ethnic churches that welcomed immigrants from many parts of the world and served as oases to support faith and culture eventually transitioned to serve wider bodies of Catholics in English; some of these churches ceased to exist as their mission ended.

If the history of U.S. Catholicism had stopped at this particular moment, we could offer this communal experience as a perfect case study of the American dream achieved. Yet history moves along. Some important changes were in store.

Before we move on, we need to understand that not all U.S. Catholics participated in this upward movement or benefitted from the wealth of resources that Euro-American Catholic communities were creating. African American, Hispanic, Native American, and Asian American Catholics largely remained on the peripheries of church and society. We cannot naively ignore the fact that sociocultural prejudices such as racism and classism have done major harm to millions of our own Catholic sisters and brothers.

Millions of Euro-American Catholics in rural areas of the country were caught up in a cycle of poverty and marginalization and were practically forgotten as the major centers of Catholic life, particularly in the urban settings of the Northeast and Midwest, thrived.

Ironically, it is these communities that inhabited the peripheries of church and society—the voices that for long were not heard, the faces that remained invisible—that are bringing new life to our faith communities and renewing the entire U.S. Catholic experience. Let me say more about this.

For the last five decades, U.S. Catholicism has been experiencing the largest demographic and cultural transformation since the time of the large migrations from Europe in the nineteenth and early twentieth centuries. Hispanics account for 71 percent of the growth of the Catholic population in the United States since 1960. Approximately 60 percent of all Catholics younger than 18 are Hispanic. The fastest-growing group in the church in this country is Asian Catholics. Hundreds of thousands of Catholics from Africa and the Caribbean have made the United States their home.

Millions of the new Catholic faces are immigrants. They bring the best of their faith and cultures to enrich our faith communities and our society. About a quarter of all Catholics in this country are immigrants. They and their children embody the hope of a new beginning. They have much to teach us about faith and life. Immigrants are neither the enemy nor a threat; they are the face of Christ, the living gospel that we are called to embrace with merciful love and Christian hospitality.

If we were to paint a broad picture of U.S. Catholics in the country, this is what the rough demographic portrait would look like: about 1 percent Native American, 4 percent African American/Black, 5 percent Asian and Pacific Islander, 40 percent Hispanic, and about 50 percent Euro-American, white. This is a much different portrait compared to, say, half a century ago when Euro-American white Catholics constituted about 85 percent to 90 percent of all Catholics in the country.

Let us look around for a moment. Turn to your right. Now to your left. Based on what we just heard, do we see the faces of present-day U.S. Catholics among us? Do we see them in our faith communities? Do we see them in our diocesan offices and organizations? Do we see them in our Catholic schools, universities, and seminaries? Are we listening to their voices? Do we know their concerns? Are we reaching out? Are they still on the peripheries of our church?

The demographic transformations of U.S. Catholicism come along with some geographical shifts that we need to keep in mind. Today, more than half of Catholics in the United States live in the South and the West. The present and the future of U.S. Catholicism is being forged in geographical regions that until now were not perceived as central to the definition of U.S. Catholic life. Today, they are!

We live in a moment in which whatever happens in Los Angeles, Houston, Atlanta, and Miami, among many other large vibrant centers of Catholic life, will likely have significant repercussions for the rest of the Catholic community nationwide. Are we paying attention?

Of concern is the fact that the rapid growth of Catholicism in the South and the West does not match the availability of resources such as parishes, schools, universities, and pastoral centers needed to support the evangelization and leadership formation of the next generation of U.S. Catholics. We are witnessing a transition from a Catholic experience highly resourced and somewhat comfortable in terms of socioeconomic positioning to one shaped strongly by Catholics with fewer resources, less education, and less emerging sociopolitical influence whose greatest treasures are their faith and their families. This is an excellent opportunity for us in this country to be a poor church for the poor, as Pope Francis reminds us, and an opportunity for solidarity among Catholics at all levels.

While contending with these demographic and geographical changes in our church, the last half a century has seen the emergence of major cultural patterns that are seriously impacting the practice of religion in our country. Among these, I want to mention four:

1. Family life has been significantly reconfigured in terms of roles, expectations, and practices. If the family is the first space where the new generations learn their faith and the matrix where faith and moral values are cultivated, Catholics must redouble our efforts to think creatively how to foster vibrant family life while responding creatively yet realistically to the challenges of being family in the United States.

2. Our society continues to witness, almost helplessly, the erosion of communal life. This has exacerbated our individualistic instincts. If communal life is not important, being with others loses meaning, advocating for others and for shared convictions is not a priority, caring about those who are most vulnerable becomes someone else's problem.

    From a religious perspective, worshiping together is not a priority anymore. It is rather disquieting that barely one-third of U.S. Catholics attend Mass on a regular basis. Even more disquieting is to know that the Catholic population has grown by about 50 percent in the last half a century, yet we find ourselves closing churches.

3. The so-called culture wars have rendered us almost unable in our society to engage in mutual and respectful dialogue. It has become impossible to speak about virtually anything

7

because it is expected that one needs to take an ideological position to make a point, and that practically means demonizing the other who somewhat disagrees with us or does not see the world as we see it. The gospel is not an ideology to be co-opted to advance any ideological position. The gospel is a message of life and communion.

4. Perhaps the most influential phenomenon impacting the practice of religion in our day is secularization: in 1991 about 6 percent of the U.S. population self-identified as nonreligiously affiliated or "nones." Today, about 25 percent of all people in our country self-identify as such. The trend is very clear. We know that about twenty million people in our country who were born and raised Catholic do not self-identify as such anymore. It is likely that many of them, especially those who are young, joined the ranks of the "nones."

About fourteen million Hispanics born and raised Catholic do not self-identify as such anymore. Most of them are young and U.S. born. Do demographic researchers count them as part of the previous twenty million? My sense is that most are not included. We have a serious challenge. Why are they leaving? Why is organized religion, particularly Catholicism, not doing it for them? Did we know that they left? If so, where is the outrage?

What do we learn from these observations? Perhaps the best way to read these realities is through the lens of two Greek terms well known in our Christian theological tradition: *krisis* and *kairos*.

Krisis is understood here in terms of transition. It is the liminal space in between what is passing and what is coming. There is no doubt that some ways of being U.S. Catholic are closing their cycle. For them we are grateful. It is fine that some Catholics feel puzzled when wrestling with diversity and pluralism, disconcerted because of a sense of loss, confused when the future does not seem as clearly defined and stable as we thought it could be—yet neither is our present.

This is where we all must exercise the pastoral practice of mutual accompaniment. It would be naive to seek a return to an idealized past, except to draw some inspiration and lessons for the future. There is no doubt that we are at the dawn of a fresher way of being Catholic in this country. At the forefront of this dawn are our young Catholic people—the majority Hispanic—with their hopes and the thirst to be church; the immigrants who bring renewed life and energy to our faith communities; the women and the men of all cultures and ages who are willing to look forward by serving as bridges to heal divides and the effects of prejudice in any of its expressions.

Yes, something new is emerging, a new time, a moment of grace, a *kairos*. We have the certainty that God walks with us and guides us with the Holy Spirit. In this *kairos* we are called to renew the invitation to proclaim the joy of the gospel in every corner of our nation. To echo the words of the prophet Ezekiel, God has called us from among the nations and gathered us from all the lands to be God's faithful people (see Ezek 36:24–28).

This is a time for Catholics in the United States not only to embrace the call to being missionary disciples but also to declare ourselves in a permanent state of mission. Let me repeat: We must declare ourselves in a permanent state of mission. We must see ourselves permanently engaged in missionary activity, going forth (*en salida*, as Pope Francis said in Spanish), taking the initiative, going to the peripheries, embracing Jesus Christ in those who are vulnerable and most in need, reaching out to those who have drifted away, accompanying and strengthening families, advocating for life in all its expressions, caring for the created order.

Hundreds of thousands of Hispanic Catholics and others modeled this commitment when they engaged in the four-year process of the Fifth National Encuentro of Hispanic/Latino Ministry. This process of evangelization was not just for Hispanics but also for the entire church in our country. Catholics across our nation were invited to join the process of the Fifth Encuentro and make it their own.

When historians one hundred years from now look back at Catholics in the United States in the first decades of the twenty-first century, we should be remembered as a generation of baptized women and men, disciples of Jesus Christ, who decided to build upon the foundations left by the previous generations, embraced the gifts of every Catholic person in our communities—without exception—and accepted to be a true evangelizing community committed to building a better society for our children and future generations of Catholics. This is our legacy.

What a wonderful time to be Catholic in the United States of America! Please join me once again in praising the Lord by saying together a resounding amen: Amen! Thank you.

2

An Immigrant Church

Timothy Matovina

The current immigration debates in the United States often reveal our collective amnesia. As immigration advocates have bemoaned, the Statue of Liberty with its shining promise of hope faces Europe, the place of origin for millions of our ancestors, but has its back to Latin America and Asia, the native lands of many of today's immigrants. Our rich U.S. Catholic heritage can enliven our faith and help us overcome our collective amnesia about our history as a predominantly immigrant church and nation.

Roman Catholics have lived their faith in what is now the United States for twice as long as the nation has existed. The oldest diocese in the New World was established in 1511 at San Juan, Puerto Rico, now a commonwealth associated with the United States. In 1565, four decades before the first British colony was established at Jamestown, Virginia, Spanish-speaking Catholics founded the first permanent European settlement within the current borders of the fifty states at St. Augustine, Florida. Before the end of the sixteenth century, Spanish Jesuits initiated missionary activities as far north as Virginia, and Franciscans established the permanent foundation of Catholicism in what is now the Southwest at El Paso, Texas. The first French Catholic settlement within current U.S. borders was on Ste. Croix (De Monts) Island in Maine and also preceded the founding of Jamestown. Spanish-speaking Black Catholics founded the first Black town in the United States, Gracia Real de Santa Teresa de Mose, in northern Florida. Asian Catholics settled in territory that is now part of the continental United States as early as the late eighteenth century, when Filipino sailors known as Manilamen abandoned Spanish galleons to begin a new life in Louisiana.

At the signing of the Declaration of Independence in 1776, scarcely 1 percent of the population in the thirteen British colonies was Catholic. Most of these Catholics were British, but some were French, German, Irish, African, or other origins. Yet within seventy-five years, Catholicism became the single largest religious denomination in the United States. The need for cheap labor coupled with conditions such as famine in Ireland and revolution in Germany coalesced to launch the largest known century of immigration to any country in recorded history. Some forty million immigrants came to the United States between the 1820s and the enactment of legislation that curtailed the immigrant flow in the 1920s. Most of these immigrants were Catholics from European backgrounds.

Large numbers did not safeguard Catholics from discrimination and hardship. Anti-Catholic literature abounded, such as Maria Monk's *Awful Disclosures of the Hotel Dieu Nunnery in Montreal* (1836), a slanderous and unfounded account of convent life that nonetheless became the best-selling literary work of its day. The prejudice fueled by such writings led to tragedies like the 1834 mob burning of an Ursuline convent and school outside of Boston. Several rioters were eventually brought to trial, but only one was convicted, and he was later pardoned. Ten years later similar mob violence in Philadelphia resulted in fourteen fatalities, numerous injuries, and the burning of two Catholic churches and the diocesan seminary.

Other adversities Catholics experienced were the lot of nearly all immigrants: leaving home and loved ones behind, adapting to life in a new land, working long hours for low pay, and dealing with frequent insults and derogatory terms. The strong U.S. patriotism of many European immigrants and their descendants is rooted in their struggles to make a life for themselves and their children and to be accepted as Americans in an often antagonistic environment.

Some Catholics suffered harm from fellow Catholics. Harsh treatment of Native Americans in the Spanish missions often led to resentment and even rebellion, most famously in the 1680 Pueblo Indian Revolt. Polish, Italian, and German Catholics frequently complained of the treatment they received from the Irish-dominated U.S. hierarchy. Some German leaders even made an unsuccessful formal appeal to the Vatican for a separate German Catholic Church in the United States. When Japanese American Catholics returned from their forced interment during World War II, they were dismayed to find their parishes closed or even demolished as part of an effort to "Americanize" them. Today we recognize the sad reality that the crisis of clergy sex abuse and bishops' transfer of offenders to new assignments devastated the lives of Catholics from all backgrounds.

African American Catholics have long suffered in the church and society. White laypeople, priests, and religious orders had slaves, many of whom were baptized Catholic and instructed in the faith but also held in bondage or sold for profit. When President Abraham Lincoln signed into law a military draft to support the northern Civil War cause in 1863, New Yorkers, many of them immigrant Irish Catholics who vied with African Americans for unskilled labor jobs, assaulted Black residents in one of the bloodiest riots in the history of the city. Augustus Tolton, a former slave who became the first African American priest, had to study in Rome because segregated U.S. seminaries would not admit him. Upon his return he faced disdain and outright hostility from white parishioners. He lived a lonely existence as an African American priest and died at the young age of forty-three. To this day, African American Catholics still toil at the arduous task of being both authentically Black and truly Catholic. The Catholic allegiance of some three million African Americans testifies to their uncommon steadfastness in the faith against all odds.

All Catholics have had heroes and saints to guide them in their struggles. The first U.S.-born canonized saint was Mother Elizabeth Ann Bayley Seton (1774–1821), who founded the first native U.S. religious community, the Daughters of Charity of St. Joseph, dedicated to Catholic education and service among the poor. She is widely acclaimed for having laid the foundation of Catholic parochial schools in the United States. Her courage, sanctity, and leadership are emblematic of an often forgotten and underappreciated group in U.S. Catholicism: the hundreds of thousands of religious sisters on whose labors and sacrifice the church was built and came to flourish.

The contributions of laywomen also span from the earliest days of American Catholic faith. One outstanding example is Saint Kateri Tekakwitha (1656–80), a child of Algonquin and Mohawk parents, born in what is now Auriesville, New York. Orphaned at age four, Tekakwitha received baptism at the age of twenty and inspired many through her life of prayer, fasting, and service to children, the elderly, and the infirmed. Devotees acclaim her as patroness of Native Americans and the environment.

Similar leadership and witness have been offered by laymen, such as Venerable Pierre Toussaint (1766–1853). Born a slave in the French colony of Saint-Domingue (Haiti), Toussaint resettled with his masters in New York, where he became a successful hairdresser to the city's aristocratic women and obtained his freedom in 1807. He lived a remarkable life of charity, securing the freedom of other enslaved persons, aiding the sick and immigrants, contributing to the education of the young and to Catholic institutions and efforts, and assisting the homeless and those in need of job training. His gifts of joy and compassion attracted the admiration of many. People from all backgrounds and walks of life attended his funeral, symbolically expressing a unity in the Eucharist that was a strikingly conspicuous countersign in that segregated time and place.

In more contemporary times, Blessed Carlos Rodríguez (1918–63) is known in his native Puerto Rico as the "lay apostle of the liturgical movement" for his translations of Catholic rites into Spanish and his commitment to catechize others about the sacraments, especially the Eucharist. Those who remember him also extol his virtue in everyday life. In the words of one admirer, he was an "ordinary man who dedicated his time to teach the name and ways of Jesus Christ."

A number of immigrant saints eased the travails of uprooted Catholic émigrés while showing the way to our true home in heaven. Saint John Nepomucene Neumann, CSsR (1811–60), was from Bohemia and of German-Czech ancestry. He spoke eight languages, was a popular preacher, and wrote two German catechisms that were widely used throughout the United States. Later he served as bishop of Philadelphia, where his organizational abilities led to a rapid expansion of parishes and parochial schools.

Italian immigrant Saint Frances Xavier Cabrini (1850–1917), the first naturalized citizen of the United States to be canonized, founded the Missionary Sisters of the Sacred Heart as well as sixty-seven Catholic institutions to care for the sick, the poor, and the abandoned. She is the patron saint of immigrants and hospital administrators. Her compatriot, Blessed Giovanni Battista Scalabrini (1839–1905), was a bishop and founder of women's and men's religious orders to serve migrants and refugees, especially the poor and those in need. Pope John Paul II proclaimed Scalabrini the "father of the immigrants."

Yet another immigrant saint was French-born Mother Theodore Guerin (1798–1856), founder of the Sisters of Providence of Saint Mary-of-the-Woods, Indiana, and several of her orders' schools. The list could go on still further: Saint Isaac Jogues, Saint Junípero Serra, Saint Rose Philippine Duchesne, Saint Damien of Moloka'i (Damien the Leper), Saint Marianne Cope of Moloka'i, and Saint Katharine Drexel, as well as Catholics whose cause for canonization is in process such as "rosary priest" Venerable Patrick Peyton, CSC, Knights of Columbus founder Venerable Father Michael McGivney, and Venerable Mother Henriette Delille, who accomplished the amazing feat of founding the Sisters of the Holy Family as an African American order of women religious in antebellum New Orleans.

The vast majority of dedicated Catholics are not officially recognized. In the 1850s, Father Thomas Cian arrived in San Francisco and became the first Chinese priest to minister in this country. Layman Daniel Rudd established the first African American Catholic newspaper and was the primary organizer for an influential series of national Black Catholic lay congresses in the late nineteenth century. Society of Helpers Sister María de la Cruz Aymes was a pioneer in Hispanic catechesis. Millions of virtually unknown faithful make up the U.S. Catholic communion of saints.

Much can be learned from the treasure of our Catholic faith in the United States. One important lesson stems from the remarkable diversity among U.S. Catholics and our rich expressions of Catholic life and devotion. More than a half century ago Dr. Martin Luther King Jr. remarked that "it is appalling that the most segregated hour of Christian America is eleven o'clock on Sunday morning, the same hour when many are standing to sing, 'In Christ there is no East or West.'" Today our increasingly diverse parishes and dioceses present a challenge and opportunity: our faith and our Catholic heritage call us to be a source of unity in a still-divided world, a countercultural light in the darkness of the numerous ways we Americans are divided from one another, even at church on Sunday morning.

Our Catholic past illuminates clear strategies for living out the admonition to be, as Saint Paul put it, neither Jew nor Greek, slave nor free, woman nor man, but rather "one in Christ Jesus" (Gal 3:28). But first we must recognize who we are. The U.S. Catholic Church is no longer an overwhelmingly immigrant church, as it was a century ago; nor is it solely an "Americanized" church as is often presumed. Rather, it is a church whose leaders at every level are primarily of European descent but with growing numbers of Latino, Asian, and African immigrants, along with sizeable contingents of native-born Latino and African American Catholics and some Native Americans.

Our ancestors in the faith teach us that the most effective strategy for building a diverse but united church is calling forth and forming leaders from all the groups that make up our church, as the varied backgrounds of our U.S. communion of saints illustrate. For example, when past church leaders complained of laxity in Italian immigrants' religious practice and with great insensitivity publicly decried the "Italian problem," the most effective response was the promotion of leadership for Italian faith communities, particularly of leaders who came from the Italian community itself, such as the Scalabrinians, Mother Cabrini's Missionary Sisters of the Sacred Heart, and Italian diocesan clergy.

This historical episode reveals that the formation of leaders cannot be confined to an old guard or some other elite group. Often, new leaders do not come forth until invited to do so. Discussion of which new leaders will be invited to formation and to specific ministries should be a consistent agenda item for parish organizations and staff at pastoral planning meetings.

Finally, we all need to become more educated about our U.S. Catholic heritage. Our spiritual reading, adult education, and courses in Catholic schools are all means to learn our history and to form ourselves in the sense that we are part of the still-unfolding story of Roman Catholicism in the United States. The heroic lives of our ancestors in the faith are a source of inspiration. Their extensive outreach and missionary endeavors induce us to evangelize, serve the needy, struggle for justice, and renew the Catholic faith of our many sisters and brothers who no longer actively participate in the church or the sacraments.

The conflicts and struggles of our forebears provide instructive counsel and remind us that current difficulties are not the first problems in the life of the church. The hills and valleys of our past refute misconceptions that pre–Vatican II Catholicism was an unchanging monolith and that the transitions of today are an aberration rather than what they actually are: the ongoing historical process of trying to live our Catholic faith in U.S. society. The recognition of our immigrant history enables us to fulfill the Lord's command to remember that we, too, "were aliens in the land" (Lev 19:34; see also Deut 10:19) and is an antidote to the collective amnesia in much of the current debates about immigration. Above all, the memory of the faith of those who went before us enables us to see God's love beyond all telling, not the "happily ever after" love of an innocent history, but divine love in the midst of the messiness of everyday life that evokes our awe, our gratitude, and our faith that we and our church are never abandoned.

3

Latino Contributions to Vatican II Renewal*

Timothy Matovina

The mutual influence of Catholicism and Latino (as well as Black, Asian, and Native) peoples in the United States is shaping not just the future of American Catholic life, but also the life of the nation. While there are many facets to the Latino presence in U.S. Catholicism, in the decades since the Second Vatican Council (1962–65) Latinos have lived out elements of the council's vision that enrich U.S. Catholicism in at least four areas: liturgy, spiritual renewal, faith and justice, and the revitalization of ecclesial life.

LITURGY

Latino worship and devotion reflect an approach that differs from the emphases among many Euro-American leaders of the liturgical renewal in the United States. Following the council, the predominant approach to the renewal accentuated the core conciliar principle of promoting the faithful's "full, conscious, and active participation" in the liturgy (*Sacrosanctum Concilium* 14). Catholic leaders in the

---

* Excerpted from the annual Charles S. Casassa, SJ, Lecture in Catholic Social Values delivered at Loyola Marymount University in Los Angeles on November 15, 2012.

United States often sought to enact this goal through emphases on the gathered assembly and the Word of God as integral elements of the Mass and other sacraments, vernacular celebration in which the priest and congregation pray in a dialogical format, and the removal of most imagery to focus attention on the altar and on the ambo from which the Scriptures are proclaimed. More recently, various Catholics have sought to restore what they perceive as a loss of reverence in parish liturgies since Vatican II, echoing a concern among a number of church leaders.

Hispanic ministry leaders have promoted additional means for fostering active participation in the liturgy. They emphasize that Vatican II enjoined pastoral leaders to respect diverse people's wisdom and pious traditions and even welcome those traditions "into the liturgy itself, so long as they harmonize with its true and authentic spirit" (*Sacrosanctum Concilium* 37). Moreover, while many Euro-American liturgical leaders underscored the council's emphasis on the "noble simplicity" (no. 34) of the Roman Rite, Latinos have insisted that this does not deter from the character of the Eucharist as a celebration, a joyful and festive prayer gathering of the church on its pilgrim way to God.

As with most aspects of U.S. Catholicism, the more dominant Euro-American influence has overshadowed that of Latinos (and other groups) in official liturgical renewal. English-speaking Catholics developed a liturgical movement well before the Second Vatican Council and led the enactment of the council's directives in the United States. Latinos were latecomers to these efforts, with no national organization dedicated specifically to liturgical renewal until they established the Instituto Nacional de Liturgia Hispana (National Institute of Hispanic Liturgy) sixteen years after the promulgation of *Sacrosanctum Concilium* in 1963. Even then Latinos had far fewer resources and less access to key leadership positions. Moreover, most Latino leaders during the pivotal decades of renewal after the council focused on what they perceived were more fundamental concerns of bolstering ministerial leadership and outreach among Latinos.

Yet the expanding contact of non-Latinos with Latino traditions has increased those traditions' influence in U.S. parishes. Parishioners and their leaders have responded to Latinos' devotional images and faith expressions in ways ranging from prohibiting or restricting them, engaging them as a means to promote causes of justice, seeing them as an inducement to recover their own ethnic Catholic traditions, or incorporating them into celebrations of the Eucharist. Through contact with Latinos a number of non-Latino Catholics have been inspired to increase their practice of Marian and other forms of piety.

Latino public rituals like those for Good Friday also draw reactions and participation from non-Latinos on the streets of a number of U.S. cities and towns. Curiosity, the devotional ambiance of the events, decisions to conduct some rituals bilingually, and non-Latinos' personal involvement with Latino communities have attracted an increasingly diverse array of participants. Even non-Catholics join in Latino public rituals. Baptist minister Buckner Fanning attested after the San Fernando Cathedral Way of the Cross procession in San Antonio that "when I walked behind Jesus on the Way of the Cross I wondered what I would have done had I been there. The people of San Fernando drew me into the passion and put me right there with Jesus."

The insufficient number of clergy and liturgical leaders who actively promote Latinos' religious traditions keeps Latino impact on communal prayer in U.S. parishes and their environs from being even greater. However, the geographic dispersion of the Latino population over the past three decades has expanded Latino influence. For good or ill, even conflicts and debates about Latino traditions and liturgical participation illuminate that Latinos shape parish worship and public ritual in significant ways. Latinos' ritual and devotional proclivities and their promotion of a liturgical renewal that engages their faith expressions currently comprise one of the fundamental dynamics in the prayer life of numerous Catholic parishes in the United States. Moreover, these dynamics and the ways pastoral leaders and non-Latino parishioners welcome, refine, or resist them transform eucharistic celebrations that are at the heart of Catholic faith and worship. The community-focused, sacramental ethos of worship and devotion in Latino communities is one of the most profound gifts they offer the wider church and society.

SPIRITUAL RENEWAL

The most conspicuous influences of Vatican II are usually per-ceived to be the structural changes in Catholic life such as the use of the vernacular in the liturgy. Yet one of the primary concerns of the council fathers was the spiritual renewal of the church, particularly in response to the new circumstances of the modern world. Concur-rent with the era of the council, apostolic movements eclipsed pious societies as the primary small faith groups among both Latinos and non-Latinos in the United States. For Latinos, these new move-ments build on the strengths of their pious society predecessors in their resonance with the devotional penchant of Latino Catholicism and their emphases on community and worthy reception of the sac-raments, but they also reflect a more widespread and explicit stress among U.S. believers on a programmatic conversion to Christianity as an intentional way of life. In fostering intense religious experi-ence, personal transformation, knowledge of one's faith, and fervor to evangelize others, apostolic movements are suited to the com-petitive religious environment of the United States and the pres-sures of modern urban life, including the unwieldy and oftentimes impersonal parish congregations in metropolitan areas.

The first large-scale apostolic movement among Latinos is the *Cursillo de Cristiandad* (Short course in Christianity) (see chapter 5). Various other Catholic apostolic movements have had noteworthy influence among Latinos and their coreligionists. Like *Cursillo*, Mar-riage Encounter (*Encuentro Matrimonial*) originated in Spain. Father Gabriel Calvo was the key leader who organized the first Encounter weekend in 1958. Calvo and Maryknoll priest Donald Hessler pro-moted the initial Encounter weekends in the United States in 1966. Subsequently, the movement spread most rapidly among English-speaking Catholics, until the following decade when Roberto and Rosie Piña of San Antonio took the initiative to expand Marriage Encounter among the Spanish-speaking.

RENEW is the most widespread program in the United States cen-tered on forming small communities to enable people and parish congregations to foster spiritual growth, integration of faith into daily life, and an evangelizing spirit. Latino Catholic emphases on family and spiritual renewal in faith communities like those formed through RENEW reflect the growing trend of Latino participation in small communities focused on Bible study and faith sharing.

The most widespread apostolic movement among Latino Catholics today is the Catholic Charismatic Renewal. Over half of parishes engaged in Hispanic ministry have Charismatic groups or activities, and literally thousands of predominantly Latino prayer groups meet regularly in parishes or private homes. Hispanic leaders established the Comité Nacional de Servicio Hispano (CNSH), also known as the Hispanic National Service Committee, in 1990 to promote the Charismatic Renewal and coordinate activities among the growing number of active Hispanic Charismatics. The CNSH has three core commitments: to serve God in the Catholic Church and advance its mission of evangelization in the power of the Holy Spirit; to foment the experience of Pentecost as a grace of the Holy Spirit for the church; and to carry the fervor of the Charismatic Renewal to families, neighborhoods, parish communities, and all those who thirst for God. One of the CNSH's major activities since its inception has been to conduct an annual leaders' training and networking meeting called the Encuentro Católico Carismático Latino de los Estados Unidos (Latino Catholic Charismatic Encounter of the United States).

Efforts such as these help to foster spiritual renewal and a missionary spirit among numerous Latino Catholics, a development that is particularly important as they confront the religious culture of choice of the United States. Addressing the prominence of the Catholic Charismatic Renewal, Allan Figueroa Deck, SJ, asserts that it "is arguably the single most important factor in the new evangelization of Hispanics and in motivating new generations of them to serve in the church as lay ministers, deacons, priests and religious." Latinos' extensive participation in apostolic movements, prayer groups, and small faith communities—indeed their pioneering efforts in creating movements like Marriage Encounter and the influential Cursillo—is one of their most significant contributions to the spiritual renewal amidst the modern world that Vatican II promoted.

FAITH AND JUSTICE

Yet another Latino contribution to the living out of Vatican II in the United States is the response to the council's often-cited call to attend to "the joys and the hopes, the griefs and the anxieties of the people of this age, especially those who are poor or in any way afflicted" (*Gaudium et spes* 1). The predominantly working-class Latino Catholic population is a widespread and visible reminder that the sometimes-harsh realities addressed in everyday pastoral work are the ordinary means through which the church lives out this mission to transform lives, communities, and society.

Currently, the most prevalent form of Catholic public presence on the timely concern of immigration is the numerous outreach efforts in local faith communities. At their best, parishes are a "safe haven" for immigrants where an array of ministries enable émigré parishioners to learn and act on their faith and provide for one another's everyday needs like food, shelter, clothing, parenting skills, family counseling, refuge from spousal abuse, employment, safe neighborhoods, English language classes, and legal defense.

When federal authorities raided the Agriprocessors factory in Postville, Iowa, on May 12, 2008, and arrested nearly four hundred undocumented workers, most of them Guatemalan and Mexican men, their wives and children fled to Saint Bridget's parish. Parish life coordinator Sister Mary McCauley, BVM, pastor emeritus Father Paul Ouderkirk, and lay Catholics, many the descendants of earlier Irish and Norwegian immigrants, served food to the frightened families, compiled a list of the detained workers, and stood watch at the church door. Immigration officials placed electronic homing devices on the ankles of about forty mothers they had detained and allowed them to reunite with their children, but the other workers faced deportation. Father Ouderkirk mourned on behalf of all: the raid "has ripped the heart out of the community and out of the parish. Probably every child I baptized has been affected. To see them stunned is beyond belief." Irma López, who was arrested along with her husband, Marcelo, but released to care for their two-year-old daughter, stated, "I came to the church because I feel safe there, I feel secure. I feel protected. I feel at peace."

The most noteworthy instance of how the expanding Latino presence has shaped the public policy positions of the U.S. Catholic Church is the bishops' solidarity with immigrants. Among Catholic bishops, immigration is the social issue that draws the most consistent public response across regions and theological perspectives, complementing the bishops' more frequently noted stance on the right to life. The bishops' collective stance on immigration perceptibly supports the contention that the Catholic defense of life extends, in the words of many Catholic leaders, across the lifespan from "conception to natural death."

The most unnoted Latino Catholic influence in promoting justice is their foundational role in shaping the faith-based model of community organizing (see chapter 5). Unlike social service efforts such as food banks and soup kitchens, faith-based community organizations focus on active citizenship rather than temporary assistance. Unlike groups that promote a defined—and in many instances single-issue—moral agenda through national and state lobbying efforts, faith-based community organizations are mediating institutions that help working-class and other congregational members participate more effectively in U.S. democratic society. These organizations offer an inherent critique of a political culture with limited nonpartisan alternatives for acting on one's faith in the political arena. The faith-based organization model that Latinos led the way in refining is one of the most effective means U.S. Catholics have contributed to advancing "the reign of justice and charity" as the council fathers at Vatican II directed (*Gaudium et spes* 76).

REVITALIZATION OF ECCLESIAL LIFE

Like their coreligionists in the United States and beyond, Vatican II's mandate for ecclesial renewal shaped the ministerial initiatives of Latino Catholic leaders. The most significant national structure for Latinos to voice their concerns and aspirations during the Vatican II era are the National Hispanic Pastoral Encuentros convened in 1972, 1977, 1985, 2000, and 2018, along with the First National Encuentro for Hispanic Youth and Young Adult Ministry in 2006. The Encuentros have been opportunities for celebration, fostering solidarity, pastoral planning, and articulating needs to bishops and other ecclesial leaders. Catholic bishops responded with various pastoral initiatives and statements, including the bishops' pastoral letter on Hispanic ministry (1983), the National Pastoral Plan for Hispanic Ministry (1987), and the 2002 statement *Encuentro and Mission: A Renewed Pastoral Framework for Hispanic Ministry*. The process of the Fifth Encuentro has provided resources for reflection and pastoral planning that various dioceses and parishes are currently using to strengthen Hispanic ministry.

While retrospective analyses of the Hispanic Pastoral Encuentros must necessarily examine the documents they produced, it is important to remember that, like all such gatherings, first and foremost the Encuentros were ecclesial events. No concluding document for such an event can fully capture the sense of solidarity among leaders coming together nationally for the first time, the power of such an ambiance to enhance creativity of pastoral and theological vision, and the courage these gatherings gave participants to break silence and form a united front to confront their experiences of injustice. Arguably the most significant, though unquantifiable, legacy of the Encuentros is their part in forming thousands of leaders who have dedicated their energies and even their life's work to the advancement of Hispanic ministry.

Many leaders avow that the Encuentros are a primary focal point for the sense of common purpose based on a shared history—what *Encuentro and Mission* calls a communal *memoria histórica* (historical memory)—that has linked various Catholics from Mexican, Puerto Rican, Cuban, and other backgrounds in Latino Catholic initiatives and organizations. The Encuentros were the symbolic center of a wide-ranging Hispanic ministry movement that shaped and was shaped by the Encuentro's own national gatherings and consultative processes. Along with U.S. bishops' efforts and pastoral statements, the Encuentros heightened recognition and respect of the Latino presence in the U.S. Catholic Church, fostered apostolic zeal for Hispanic ministry, and advocated for the expansion of resources and personnel dedicated to that work.

Moreover, the Encuentros are the most conspicuous means by which Hispanics have engaged in conversations and debates about the renewal of Catholicism in the United States since Vatican II. Drawing on the teachings of the council, the Latin American bishops in their postconciliar conferences beginning at Medellín, and the popes, the conclusions of the Hispanic Pastoral Encuentros proposed core pastoral and theological precepts for the enhancement both of Hispanic ministry and of ecclesial life in U.S. Catholicism. Prominent among these precepts are respect for diverse languages, cultures, and faith traditions as part of the beauty of God's creation; the commitment to evangelization and justice as constitutive of the church's mission to proclaim Jesus Christ; the urgency to serve and foster leadership among marginal groups such as farm workers, women, young people, immigrants, and the wider Hispanic population; and the call to transform personal lives as well as cultures, society, and the internal dynamics of the church itself.

Underlying these convictions is a core ecclesiology, an understanding of the church as the Body of Christ incarnate among people in the reality of their everyday lives. This perspective echoes the Vatican II statement that "the church... must implant itself among all these groups in the same way that Christ by his incarnation committed himself to the particular social and cultural circumstances of the women and men among whom he lived" (*Ad Gentes* 10). Underscoring the church as a community charged to embody Christ's presence in the concrete circumstances of human life, the Encuentro vision encapsulates the theological foundation that has animated Hispanic ministry leaders in their collective efforts to transform Catholicism in the United States through their pastoral planning and action during the Vatican II era.

The Vatican II era in U.S. Catholicism is often depicted as one of conflict between progressives and conservatives, or as a debate about whether interpretations of the council should highlight continuity or discontinuity with previous councils and church teaching. Although Latinos have not participated extensively in these disputes, the impact of Vatican II in the United States cannot be fully understood without an assessment of Latino contributions.

Latino initiatives are not merely part of the recent history of U.S. Catholicism but are also integral to its present and its future. Most importantly, these Latino initiatives remind us that, while the interpretation of the council documents is crucial, no examination of the Vatican II era is complete without understanding the ways that the council inspired Catholics in the United States—and elsewhere—to revitalize their faith, worship, ecclesial life, and evangelizing mission. The significance of Vatican II is not found merely in its proceedings, but in illuminating how Latino and other Catholics have cooperated with God's grace to transform our lives, our church communities, and our world in light of the council.

4

Called and Sent to Encuentro*

Hosffman Ospino

LISTENING TO GOD'S CALL

The God of life, who by the power of the Holy Spirit conquered death, sin, and darkness through the resurrection of Jesus Christ, our Lord, calls Hispanic Catholics in the United States with a renewed impetus to be *pueblo de Dios en marcha*. In God who is three in one we believe. To God who is origin and wellspring of our existence we give our praise. In God who walks with us in the confines of history we place our trust and our hope as we enter into this process leading to the Fifth National Encuentro of Hispanic/Latino Ministry, truly a moment of grace.

God rejoices in the beauty of the created order. God finds delight in the people from all cultures who live according to the truth, particularly the truth of the gospel, and love with *caritas*: God's divine love. The United States of America is our share of creation. This is our land, our nation.

---

* Pastoral theological vision delivered as a keynote on October 30, 2014, in San Antonio, Texas, to launch the process of the Fifth National Encuentro of Hispanic/Latino Ministry and used nationwide to train tens of thousands of leaders engaged in the process.

This is where we find ourselves walking side by side with millions of people who believe that life is about opportunity, people who strive every day to build a better world. This is where we find ourselves walking together with God, who not only called us into being but also promised to accompany us along the journey. Here we live.

Most of us were born in this nation; many others were reborn as migrants. In a land that promises new beginnings, we find ourselves participating in a never-ending process of rebirthing, re-creating, reinventing, renewing.

Our *experiencia cotidiana* as Christian disciples living in the United States is often complex, busy, noisy, tense. Much is negotiated at any given moment. Many realities change so fast around us that we barely have time to remember what was and contemplate what is. Notwithstanding, we have the responsibility to imagine a shared future. Communities, large and small, change. Priorities change. Political dynamics, global and local, change.

How we enter in relationship with God changes as well as how we practice our faith. We change. Yet amid the drumming that engulfs life with its many changes, God invites us today to pause for a moment and ponder about who we are as women and men called to *Encuentro* here and now.

WE ARE HISPANIC...

Hispanic, *Latino/a*, Latin@, *indígena*, Hispanic American....Yes, all of the above. We are all these and many more. Our people are brown, black, white, mestizo, mulatto....When exercising our democratic responsibilities we vote all across the political spectrum. We are professionals, businesspeople, educators, artists, service workers, *campesinos*.

Many among us trace our lineage to families who have lived in the United States for centuries, even to ancestors who lived in the land before the country knew itself as a nation. Others more recently crossed borders, flew in, and sailed boats from Latin America and the Caribbean with the hope of finding better opportunities for them and their families.

Although millions among our people are immigrants who have made this country their permanent home in recent decades, we are not just an immigrant community. The vast majority, nearly two-thirds of *nuestro pueblo*, were born in the United States. We are Hispanic, *Latino/a*, Latin@, *indígenas*, and…American, that is, *estadounidenses*. This is our country. We are the United States along with many others who day by day work hard and long to build a better nation.

We believe in dreams that inspire us as a people. We dream about building strong families in which parents, children, spouses, grandparents, uncles and aunts, cousins, *comadres* and *compadres*, and the many other relatives and friends who are part of our lives are always welcomed. We dream about the best education and opportunities for our children so they can live their lives to the fullest.

We dream that the honor that derives from affirming the dignity of our human condition, an honor that has been denied to many of us, particularly our women and our children in the countries that many of us have left, and even in this land, is fully restored as we build a new society. We dream that our lives be filled with joy and peace as we trust in the Lord.

Poverty, low educational attainment, brokenness in our families, large numbers of our sisters and brothers in prisons and detention centers, the hardships that are part of the immigrant experience, among other trials, negatively affect the lives of millions of our Hispanic sisters and brothers, especially the young, in our barrios and homes. Racism and classism are persistent social biases that some in this society, our society, inflict again and again upon us as a *pueblo* because of the consistent failure to understand who we are and what we contribute to church and society. When one of us suffers because of those biases, we all suffer, the church suffers, the country suffers. Yet we still dream.

Our shared history is like a colorful tapestry weaved over five centuries, a tapestry made of multiple narratives that are part of one common memory: *nuestra memoria histórica*. Many of these great narratives evoke moments that have brought hope and the promise of new beginnings. Others remind us of the clashes that have caused pain and despair.

It is in the walking together through history, motivated by the passions that drive us every day, mindful of the joys and hopes, the grief and anguish of our people, that a new identity is being forged. Not an identity that does away with differences, diversity of cultures, national origins, accents, and memories—because without these we would not be who we are today—but an identity that has the power to hold unity and plurality in dynamic tension.

Many ask when is it that the process of forging such identity will finally be completed. Are we there yet? All we can say is that we are still being born. For centuries, we have been becoming something new; we are not done. We are becoming something new and so are the people with whom we live, our neighborhoods, the towns and cities where we are *presente*, the larger society, the church.

WE ARE HISPANIC CATHOLICS...

At the heart of the always-evolving U.S. Hispanic identity, in all its variations and manifestations, remains a spiritual constant: Christianity, particularly mediated by Catholicism. Most Hispanics in the United States still self-identify as Catholic.

The Catholic experience has served perhaps as the most widely shared quality among Hispanic and Latin American peoples in the continent. Rooted in the experience of Iberian Catholicism, the church throughout our history in the United States, the Caribbean, and in the rest of the continent has been a major force shaping culture, education, the arts, and social life. Hispanics are heirs of this tradition, and we carry it in what many have come to recognize as a form of cultural Catholicism.

The Hispanic Catholic experience is a treasure that permeates the life of the church in the United States and the larger society in many ways. For decades, theologians and pastoral leaders in this country, the Caribbean, and Latin America have recognized the immense power of popular Catholicism as a vehicle not only to celebrate and interpret the faith but also to pass on that faith from one generation to the next. Marian devotions, especially the love for Our Lady of

Guadalupe, have a special place in the U.S. Hispanic Catholic imagination.

Liturgical life remains important for Hispanic Catholics. Parishes where Hispanics are present tend to have a higher number of faithful attending Mass, and the number of children baptized in these communities is higher than in the rest of parishes in the country. Of course, the record is not perfect, and much more needs to be done at the pastoral level to help the many Hispanic Catholics who sporadically or never come to church to appreciate more the richness of its liturgical experience. Yet there is a sense of the sacred, what theologians call a sacramental imagination, deeply ingrained in Hispanic cultures, much of it nurtured by the centuries-long relationship with Catholicism.

In recent decades, the emergence of the apostolic movements (e.g., the Catholic Charismatic Renewal, *Cursillo*) has inspired waves of spiritual revitalization among U.S. Hispanic Catholics. All these experiences point to what has been identified as *mística*, that lens through which Hispanic Catholics see and understand the world as a place where it is always possible to have an encounter with the divine.

For Hispanic Catholics, the experience of *encuentro* is an opportunity to retrieve the cultural, spiritual, and ecclesial roots of our shared identity. In Latin America and the Caribbean, the spirit of *encuentro* has, without a doubt, shaped the pastoral theological reflection of CELAM (*Consejo Episcopal Latinoamericano*) for more than half a century. The meetings in Medellín (1968), Puebla (1979), Santo Domingo (1992), and most recently in Aparecida (2007) can be considered *encuentro* milestones. At these meetings pastoral leaders and theologians from around the continent came together (*se encontraron*) to reflect on how God's reign was being experienced by *el pueblo*, the people.

Those experiences of *encuentro* in Latin America have inspired some of the most exciting processes of pastoral planning, parish renewal, and missionary activity in our recent history. Many of the twenty million immigrants from Latin America and the Caribbean now living in the United States have been formed and transformed by those dynamics: catechists, teachers, lay pastoral agents, vowed religious, clergy, and countless people in the pews. As we enter the process leading toward the Fifth Encuentro, their experiences and memories should be a great source of inspiration.

WE ARE HISPANIC CATHOLICS IN THE UNITED STATES...

At the time of the Second Vatican Council (1962–65), Hispanics constituted less than 10 percent of the Catholic population in the United States. In a church that was mostly Euro-American, Hispanic Catholics were clearly a minority. This is how we had been perceived for quite a long time.

As a minority, the history of Hispanics had been influenced by the ups and downs of the racial, social, and even religious tensions that dominated major conversations in the larger society, but much has changed in only half a century. Today, Hispanics constitute more than 40 percent of all Catholics in the country. More than half of Catholics under the age of twenty-five are Hispanic. Seventy-one percent of the growth of Catholicism in the country since the 1960s is the result of the Hispanic presence. It is practically impossible in our day to speak about the present and future of Catholicism in the United States without looking closely at the Hispanic Catholic experience.

Has the church in the United States come to terms with the process of Hispanicization that is currently redefining its identity? Are Hispanic Catholics aware of the role we now play and the commitments we must assume in the context of the new phase in the U.S. Catholic experience? The Fifth Encuentro process is the perfect opportunity to reflect upon these two questions.

This is not the first time we enter into a process of *encuentro*. Prior to the present Fifth Encuentro process, Hispanic Catholics have been part of several other *Encuentros Nacionales Hispanos de Pastoral*: 1972, 1977, 1985, and 2000. In 2006, the First National Encuentro for Hispanic Youth and Young Adult Ministry took place. The Encuentros have been instances of communal reflection where pastoral leaders involved in Hispanic ministry came together through a series of processes and gatherings at various levels to address how the church in the United States is best meeting the pastoral and spiritual needs and aspirations of Hispanic Catholics.

The Encuentros quickly proved to be prophetic moments, but perhaps their most important contribution has been the development of a shared consciousness among U.S. Hispanic Catholics. The first three Encuentros focused explicitly on the Hispanic Catholic experience. In doing so, they named the strengths and weaknesses in the church's response to the growing Hispanic presence.

The Third Encuentro (1985) was preceded by a two-year (1983–85) process of consultation at multiple levels involving hundreds of thousands of Hispanic Catholics. The Third Encuentro also inspired the development of the 1987 National Pastoral Plan for Hispanic Ministry, approved by the bishops of the United States for all Catholics in the country. The plan's general objective continues to inspire major initiatives and conversations about Hispanic ministry nationwide:

> To live and promote, by means of a *pastoral de conjunto*
> a model of the church that is communitarian, evangeliz-
> ing and missionary, incarnate in the reality of the Hispanic
> people and open to the diversity of cultures, a pro-
> moter and example of justice... that develops leadership
> through integral education... that is leaven for the king-
> dom of God in society.

Encuentro 2000 (considered the Fourth Encuentro) raised awareness about the gift of diversity in the church. It was not focused exclusively on Hispanic ministry, yet it was an opportunity for Hispanics to share the experience and methodology of *encuentro* with other Catholics in the country. The First National Encuentro for Hispanic Youth and Young Adult Ministry not only reminded us that Hispanic Catholic youth must remain a central focus in the church's evangelizing mission in the United States (about six in ten Catholics under the age of eighteen in the country are Hispanic), but also demonstrated the capacity and potential for leadership of U.S. young Hispanic Catholics.

Today, about sixty million Hispanics, 17 percent of the entire U.S. population, constitute a major force in our society. Hispanics are present in every state, every major urban center throughout the country. Hardly a group to be ignored!

Nearly thirty million of us self-identify as Catholics. There are more Hispanic Catholics in the United States than in most individual countries in Latin America.

This is without a doubt a different moment in our shared history. Our reflection at this time is not merely about how the larger ecclesial community can serve a small group of people who share common languages and cultures. It is about embracing the fact that Catholicism in the United States is being—and will continue to be—deeply redefined by the Hispanic Catholic experience in dialogue with the many other Catholic experiences that are part of the culturally diverse matrix in which we hear and answer God's calling to *encuentro*.

WE ARE HISPANIC CATHOLICS IN THE UNITED STATES IN THE TWENTY-FIRST CENTURY...

As we move forward as a church well into the second decade of the still-young twenty-first century, Hispanic Catholics insist that our challenges, questions, and hopes are those of the church in the United States—and vice versa. Every historical moment brings its own challenges, and every challenge is in itself a new opportunity.

At the dawn of this century our society experienced the horrors of terrorism and large-scale violence. These events profoundly changed our perception about the kind of world in which we live today. A new wave of sociopolitical crises in Latin America threatens the well-being of many, especially women and the young, leaving them no other alternative than to flee their homelands. Many look North as an option, as did millions throughout the twentieth century.

Recent economic downturns underscore the vulnerability of the institutions in which we have come to rely almost blindly. A growing anti-immigrant sentiment, particularly during times of political elections, reveals worrisome xenophobic attitudes in our society that need to be seriously addressed. This seems to be a time when turning to God and religious institutions for guidance and wisdom is more urgent than ever, yet our society collectively is moving in a different direction: secularism. About 25 percent of people in the United States self-identify as nonreligiously affiliated, or "nones." Hispanics are not the exception.

These are precisely the conversations where Hispanic Catholics can lead with our voices, witness, and leadership. These are our realities as well. This is our time to be a prophetic voice! Our children and grandchildren are growing up in this context. The response to these dynamics is what in many ways will determine the vibrancy and relevance of our parishes, dioceses, organizations, and institutions.

In order to respond to the challenges of our day, we stand before a unique opportunity to draw from the best of our Catholic tradition as well as from the richness of our cultural and historical experiences. We are Hispanic Catholics in the United States in the twenty-first century who accept God's call to *encuentro* and stand ready to make preferential options. We continue to embrace the preferential option for the poor that has characterized the church in Latin America and the Caribbean as well as Hispanic ministry in the United States during the last half a century.

We know the effects of poverty firsthand because millions of our people suffer due to the conditions created by this social ill. Many struggle for jobs to support their families while others receive unreasonably low wages for their hard work. For many, promotion in the workplace is a chimera while they see their co-workers who work as hard and have similar qualifications achieve higher levels of success.

Lack of access to quality education and education that effectively moves our young up the social scale, particularly in urban settings, practically condemns many of our people to live in poverty for the rest of their lives. Disproportionate rates of imprisonment in comparison

Sell your books at
sellbackyourBook.com!

Go to sellbackyourBook.com
and get an instant price quote.
We even pay the shipping - see
what your old books are worth
today!

000440124321

to the rest of the population; the proliferation of detention centers to confine immigrants largely from Latin America, including mothers and children; and a large number of Hispanics paying long sentences in regular prison systems add an extra burden on the shoulders of families that seek a better chance in life, especially for their young. These are our people, and these are our struggles. With them we elevate our voices to the God of life who hears the cry of the poor (see Ps 34:6; 69:33; Job 34:28).

We also renew the preferential option for our Hispanic youth. The majority of U.S. Catholics under the age of thirty are Hispanic, most of them born in this country. There is plenty of evidence that our ministerial structures, including parish youth and young adult ministerial programs, Catholic schools, and Catholic colleges are not doing enough to serve them well. If we do not invest in Hispanic youth now, what kind of church do we expect to have in ten or twenty years? Investment in Hispanic youth today is nonnegotiable.

As we enter the process of the Fifth Encuentro, we must make a preferential option for the family, more specifically the Hispanic family. Hispanic Catholics in general have a strong sense of family life and value the importance of this social unit. The openness to life in Hispanic families, expressed particularly in the number of children at home, serves as a countercultural sign to what some have identified the "culture of death" in our society. Hispanic families, rooted in the conviction that individual identity is primarily shaped in the context of the home, remain by and large paradigmatic in terms of sharing traditional values about culture, faith, and mores. These strengths should be cultivated in our ministry and shared with others as much as possible as Hispanics continue to grow roots in this society.

However, it is easy to confuse "a strong sense of family" with an idealized view of the Hispanic family. Hispanic families also struggle significantly. Yes, there is brokenness in our families. There is pain when our families are divided because of migratory policies that are taking too long to be revised. There is grief when marriages in our communities fail. There is hardship when our families must permanently deal with poverty and marginalization.

There is frustration among our parents when they dream about the best education for their children and know that millions of their little ones go to failing schools that put their future at risk. There is reason to be concerned when realities like machismo, domestic violence, and other forms of domestic abuse directly affect the lives of many in our families, particularly women and children, yet are often met with a deafening silence by leaders in our faith communities.

There is confusion when our own ministerial structures, including current efforts in Hispanic ministry, invest little or nothing in *pastoral familiar*. If we do not invest in Hispanic families now, what kind of church do we expect to have in ten or twenty years? Investment in the Hispanic family today is nonnegotiable.

SENT BY GOD AS MISSIONARY DISCIPLES...

As the church throughout the world continues to embrace the call to the new evangelization, Hispanic Catholics do so in our day in a spirit of *encuentro*. Saint Paul VI reminded us that the church exists to evangelize (*Evangelii Nuntiandi* 14). Hispanic ministry in the United States only makes sense if its goal is to announce the good news of Jesus Christ.

As Hispanic Catholics and those walking with us in a mutual spirit of accompaniment, we have heard the voice of the God of life who calls us to discipleship. We follow in the footsteps of the Lord Jesus, the risen One who makes all things new. We open our hearts to the guidance of the Holy Spirit for our discipleship to be authentic and life-giving. Hispanic ministry in the United States is the church's commitment to bringing the good news of Jesus Christ with new ardor, new methods, and new expressions to all Hispanic women and men living in this land, those who walk with us in our communities and those with whom we are church amid the cultural diversity that shapes our communal identity.

Christian discipleship is about following Jesus, the teacher. Yet the act of following must be preceded by a moment of listening and contemplation. At the feet of the Lord Jesus, like the first disciples, we listen to his words and our hearts are filled with the joy of the gospel (*Evangelii Gaudium* 1).

We contemplate the truth that makes us free. We humbly allow the Lord to love us with the sacrificial love of the one who lays his life down for his friends. The *encuentro* with the Lord through his word in the Scriptures, his sacraments, and our neighbors, especially those most vulnerable (see Matt 25:31–46), empowers us to say with the author of the First Letter of John, "We declare to you what we have seen and heard so that you also may have fellowship with us" (1 John 1:3a).

The proclamation of the good news inherently implies a movement outward. If we have seen it, heard it, and contemplated it, we know how worthy it is! Then we must share it. Authentic discipleship and the church's missionary impetus go hand in hand. As the pastoral leaders from across the continent who gathered in Aparecida, Brazil, in 2007 concluded, this is the time to embrace our identity as missionary disciples.

The call to missionary discipleship clearly resonates with the pastoral experience of U.S. Hispanic Catholics. For decades we have been in close dialogue with theological and pastoral movements from Latin America. Many of those movements have profoundly influenced our own reflection as is the case of the earlier *Encuentros Nacionales Hispanos de Pastoral*. The 1997 synod that led to the landmark document *Ecclesia in America* modeled how the conversation could continue.

Much energy is being generated in the Latin American ecclesial context inspired by Aparecida, the commitment to a continental mission, and without a doubt the witness of Pope Francis, the first Latin American pope in history. This is truly a *kairos* moment for U.S. Hispanic, Latin American, and Caribbean Catholics, a time to embrace the calling to be missionary disciples. This is an opportunity to be missionary to all our sisters and brothers, Hispanic and non-Hispanic, in the United States. As U.S. Hispanic Catholics, we enter this moment rooted in our own reality, yet mindful of the need to develop a wider awareness of the experiences beyond our own boundaries and most immediate perspectives.

TO EXPERIENCE THE FULLNESS OF GOD'S LOVE THROUGH *ENCUENTRO!*

Catholicism in the United States in the twenty-first century will be profoundly defined by whether and how we build communities of *encuentro* and embrace. It is in these communities where everyone, Hispanic and non-Hispanic, should find ourselves at home and experience the fullness of God's love. This is a time when Catholic parishes, dioceses, organizations, and institutions are to renew their commitment to identity and mission by becoming spaces where all Catholics are welcomed with their gifts, questions, and hopes.

To build such communities it is necessary to develop a *pastoral de conjunto* that builds on the best practices that have given life to many communities to this day. This *pastoral de conjunto* also requires the incorporation of the wisdom that new pastoral leaders, young and old, immigrant and U.S. born, Hispanic and non-Hispanic, bring to our communities.

Pope Francis often refers to the idea of fostering a *cultura de encuentro* (a culture of encounter). A culture of encounter brings people together mirroring the *encuentro* between God and humanity, particularly through Jesus Christ. Such an encounter is always life-giving and transforming. It is an encounter that affirms the best of who we are as people created and loved by God.

A culture of encounter is predicated upon the conviction that forgiveness and reconciliation are possible. It is a culture that speaks the truth with clarity, although with kindness and mercy. A culture of encounter mediates differences, brings together those who are alienated from each other, heals conflicts, and opens us up to the beauty of the mystery of being together with one another. Yes, we are in this as a *pueblo*. We are the church, *el pueblo de Dios*.

The process of the Fifth National Encuentro of Hispanic/Latino Ministry should be seen by Hispanic pastoral leaders and those who accompany us on the journey of building strong communities of faith as an invitation to foster *una cultura de encuentro* that makes it possible for all to experience the fullness of God's reign. May the God of life, who by the power of the Holy Spirit calls us to follow our Lord Jesus Christ as missionary disciples and accompany one another on this journey of fashioning the U.S. Catholic experience in the twenty-first century, grant us the wisdom to remain faithful to our vocation.

5

Ten Things to Know about Hispanic Catholics

Timothy Matovina

The growing Hispanic presence is transforming U.S. Catholic life. Here are ten basic facts that many Catholics do not know about the people who now make up more than 40 percent of the church in the United States.

1. HISPANICS WERE THE FIRST ROMAN CATHOLICS IN WHAT IS NOW THE UNITED STATES.

Spanish-speaking Catholics have lived in what is now the United States for twice as long as the nation has existed. The first diocese in the New World was established in 1511 at San Juan, Puerto Rico, now a commonwealth associated with the United States. Catholic subjects of the Spanish Crown founded the first permanent European settlement within the current borders of the fifty states at St. Augustine, Florida, in 1565, four decades before the establishment of the first British colony at Jamestown. In 1598, Spanish subjects traversed present-day El Paso, Texas, and proceeded north to establish the permanent foundation of Catholicism in what is now the Southwest.

Because of this long-standing presence, the first large group of Hispanic Catholics became part of the United States without ever leaving home, as they were incorporated into its boundaries during U.S. territorial expansion into Florida and then westward. Hispanic Catholics settled in Nacogdoches, Texas, for example, in 1716. In 1834, a Protestant newcomer murdered the local Catholic pastor, Father José Antonio Díaz de León, though an Anglo-American judge exonerated him on the outrageous defense that this revered priest had committed suicide. The new U.S. settlers drove many other Mexican residents from their lands and burned the Catholic church building to the ground. Yet when a replacement for Father Díaz de León finally arrived thirteen years after the murder, the new priest was amazed to find that for all those years Mexican Catholics had continued to gather in private homes for Sunday worship, feast days, and catechesis of their children. Such instances of Hispanics' faith and endurance in the conquered territories of the Southwest are one of the most frequently overlooked chapters in U.S. Catholic history.

2. HISPANICS ARE A DIVERSE GROUP.

A growing number of Hispanics are in the middle or even upper classes, but most are a poor or working-class population who face daily hardships, such as a lack of opportunities in education and employment, inadequate healthcare, and general strain on family cohesion and personal well-being. Regional and generational differences further contribute to the tremendous diversity among U.S. Hispanics, as do the national backgrounds from which they or their ancestors originate. Today, Spanish is a primary language in twenty-two countries, all of which have native daughters and sons residing in the United States, the second largest and most diverse Spanish-speaking nation in the world. About two-thirds of the sixty million

Hispanics in the United States are ethnically Mexicans, but there are also significant numbers from Puerto Rican, Cuban, Dominican, and Central American backgrounds, along with some South Americans and a growing number from "mixed" Hispanic parentages.

Pastoral leaders need to be aware of the different religious traditions, customs, and even Spanish words of Hispanic groups. At St. Cecilia parish in New York, during the mid-1990s when newly arrived Mexican émigrés enshrined their national patroness, Our Lady of Guadalupe, in a niche within the church, their fellow parishioners pressed for equally prominent displays of their own Marian images. Puerto Ricans honored their patroness, Nuestra Señora de la Divina Providencia, and Ecuadorans Nuestra Señora de El Cisne. Their pastor wisely guided this "renewed interest in patron saints" as a means to build unity and a greater sense of belonging among all parishioners. Effective pastoral leadership like this is needed to address the potential for ethnic rivalry, especially when one Hispanic group is numerically larger than others in a parish.

3. MOST HISPANICS ARE NOT IMMIGRANTS.

Immigration is a hot topic for many Americans, including Catholics. Among our bishops, immigration is the social issue that draws the most consistent response across regions and theological perspectives, complementing the bishops' more frequently noted defense of the right to life. Archbishop José Gomez of Los Angeles reflects the view of many in his assertion that immigration is "the greatest civil rights test of our generation." Yet most Latinos—some two-thirds—are not immigrants. Immigration debates, as essential as they are, often blind us to the staggering demographic reality of Hispanic generational transition: over the next three decades the number of third-generation Hispanics will triple, the second generation will double, and the overall percentage (though not necessarily the raw numbers) of first-generation immigrants will decline. Hispanics are a very young group compared to the rest of the U.S.

population, and they already comprise more than half of U.S. Catholics under the age of twenty-five.

The transition from immigrant to U.S.-born or U.S.-reared generations is at the heart of the evangelization challenge among Hispanics. As they begin to surpass their parents' and grandparents' often-limited formal education, young Hispanics need catechesis that engages their minds as well as their hearts. Most young Hispanics are fluent in English, which in many instances causes communication difficulties with Spanish-dominant parents. Often the faith of their elders does not adequately address the complex reality of the world in which young people live. They need formation in the Catholic faith and teachings that both address that reality and build on their elders' religious traditions. While immigrants and their needs are crucial, passing on the Catholic faith to young Hispanics is an even more urgent priority for the entire U.S. Catholic Church. How we address this priority today in families, Catholic schools, catechetical programs, and youth ministries will in large part determine what our church will be tomorrow.

4. HISPANICS HAVE DEEP DEVOTION TO JESUS AND TO HIS EUCHARISTIC PRESENCE.

Most U.S. Catholics are aware of Hispanic devotion offered in places like Mexico's famous shrine to Our Lady of Guadalupe. Far fewer are aware that nearly half the shrines dedicated to miraculous images in colonial Mexico focused on an image of Christ. Hispanic traditions during the Advent and Christmas season enable them to accompany Mary and Joseph on the way to Jesus's birthplace at Bethlehem (*posadas*), place the child Jesus in the crib (*acostada del niño*), worship at the manger scene (*nacimiento*), process with the Magi (*los santos reyes*), and especially in Puerto Rican communities, honor family and friends with an unexpected choral visit to their homes (*parrandas navideñas*). Latinos also accompany Jesus on Good Friday through the Way of the Cross (*Viacrucis*), the seven last words of Christ (*siete palabras*), his entombment (*servicio del santo entierro*), and in a wake service at which he is remembered and his sorrowful mother consoled (*pésame*).

The U.S. bishops offered a profound reflection on such devotions in their 1983 pastoral, *The Hispanic Presence: Challenge and Commitment*: "Hispanic spirituality places strong emphasis on the humanity of Jesus, especially when he appears weak and suffering, as in the crib and in his passion and death" (no. 12). The desire for intimate contact with Jesus is also evident in Hispanic devotion to the Blessed Sacrament. Whether in Corpus Christi processions, the altar of repose on Holy Thursday, nocturnal adoration, or a simple visit before the tabernacle in a parish church, numerous Hispanics have a keen sense of Christ's real eucharistic presence as Lord and brother.

5. HISPANIC CULTURES ARE FOCUSED ON COMMUNITY.

Numerous Spanish-language *dichos* (sayings or proverbs) underscore the conviction that people are profoundly shaped and known through their relationships. For example, one popular expression is "Dime con quién andas y te diré quién eres" (Tell me with whom you walk, and I will tell you who you are). As one Hispanic woman told me, "For the Hispanic, we cannot know someone without knowing their family. The first question we ask when we meet someone is 'Where are you from? Who is your family?'" Rooted in the Catholic influence on Latin American life and cultures across centuries, this focus on community is often expressed in practical solidarity like Hispanics' opening their homes to others, sharing even the little they have, and their concern for the well-being of family, friends, and even strangers. It is also expressed in Hispanics' joy, spontaneity, and affectivity, which enrich parish events and worship in numerous U.S. Catholic congregations.

Hispanic faith expressions are imbued with this community-focused understanding of the human person. In the face of emphases on the autonomous individual in modern cultures, Hispanic devotions highlight relationships like those between Jesus and Mary. The presence of both Jesus and Mary in traditional Hispanic Good Friday rituals, for example, reveals the mutual love of mother and son that death cannot break. Mary and Jesus walk together in their hour of gravest need, while devotees walk along and ritually imitate what mother and son did at the first Way of the Cross in Jerusalem. Theologian Roberto Goizueta says their prayers express a "theology of accompaniment": Hispanic devotees accompany Jesus and Mary in prayer with unwavering confidence that their savior and his loving mother will also accompany them in their daily lives and struggles. This community-focused dimension of Hispanic prayer is conducive to celebrating the Eucharist as a communion between God and all of humankind and thus is especially important for priests, deacons, and other liturgical ministers who lead Hispanics in sacramental worship.

6. HISPANICS FOUNDED THE MOST INFLUENTIAL RETREAT MOVEMENT IN THE COUNTRY.

Eduardo Bonnín and other Spanish laymen in Mallorca, Spain, established the *Cursillo de Cristiandad* (Short Course in Christianity) in the wake of World War II. In 1957, two of their countrymen assigned to a Waco, Texas, military base collaborated with Father Gabriel Fernández to lead the first *Cursillo* weekend retreat in the United States. Four years later, *Cursillo* team members from previous Spanish-language weekends led the first English-language *Cursillo*. By the following year *Cursillistas* had conducted weekends in such places as San Francisco, Chicago, Detroit, Cincinnati, Baltimore, and Boston.

Over the ensuing two decades, nearly every diocese in the United States introduced the *Cursillo* movement, impacting literally millions of Catholics from a variety of backgrounds. As *Cursillo* spread, a number of retreat programs that closely emulate its core dynamics appeared: Teens Encounter Christ (TEC), Search (and its Spanish counterpart *Búsqueda*), Kairos, Christ Renews His Parish, and the Protestant Walk to Emmaus and youth-oriented Chrysalis retreats, among others. Thus the Hispanic-founded *Cursillo* had far-reaching impact on other Catholics and even on Protestants, making it the most influential weekend retreat movement in the United States.

7. HISPANICS PIONEERED THE FAITH-BASED MODEL OF COMMUNITY ORGANIZING.

While African Americans forged church involvement in social transformation through the Civil Rights movement, Saul Alinsky's organizing model, developed in his well-known work in the Back of the Yards neighborhood in Chicago beginning in the late 1930s, has been among the most influential broad-based community organizing efforts in the United States. The first predominantly Hispanic faith-based community organization, San Antonio's Communities Organized for Public Service (COPS), played a key role in transforming Alinsky's organizing model to root it more deeply in local congregations and the faith of their members. Organizer Ernie Cortés worked with lay leaders and priests to establish COPS among ethnic Mexican Catholic parishes in the working-class neighborhoods of the city's west side.

COPS members learned from Alinsky's organizing model, but as Hispanic Catholics they also infused Alinsky's style of organizing with the faith of their core leaders: parishioners who perceived their activism as an extension of their commitment to God, church, family, and neighborhood. The COPS approach of building a community organization on the foundation of congregations and faith-based leaders has been adapted and further developed in various forms in faith-based community organizations, which now exist in nearly every state.

8. A GROWING NUMBER OF HISPANICS ARE IN THE CANONIZATION PROCESS.

Like the wider Hispanic Catholic population, those in the process of canonization include both immigrants and U.S.-born Hispanics. Pope John Paul II beatified Carlos Manuel Rodríguez Santiago (1918–63) in 2001, advancing him to the final stage before canonization. Blessed Carlos is known in his native Puerto Rico for his virtue, his love of the liturgy, his translations of Catholic rites into Spanish, and his commitment to teach others about the sacraments, especially the Eucharist. He is the first layperson born in a territory of the United States to be beatified. Father Félix Varela y Morales (1788–1853) is among those declared venerable, the step before beatification in the canonization process. When the Spanish regime condemned him to death in 1823 because of his support of Cuban independence, he fled to New York and worked as a parish priest and eventually as diocesan vicar general. He is recognized as a forerunner of Cuban pro-independence thought and for his dedicated pastoral service in New York. Bishop Alphonse Gallegos (1931–91) is in the initial stage of the canonization process. He was born in Albuquerque, joined the Augustinian Recollects, and served as auxiliary bishop in the Diocese of Sacramento, California, for the last decade of his life. His cause for sainthood was opened fourteen years after his tragic death from a car that struck him as he tried to push his stalled vehicle to the roadside.

In 2015, Franciscan priest Junípero Serra (1713–84) became the first Hispanic who served in territories of the United States to be canonized a saint. Pope Francis canonized Father Serra, acclaiming his holiness and apostolic labors as the founder of the missions in California. The canonization causes of still other missioners of Spain in territories now part of the United States are currently active: Venerable Antonio Margil de Jesús, OFM (1657–1726), in Texas; Servant of God Eusebio Kino, SJ (1645–1711), in Arizona; groups of Franciscan and Jesuit martyrs who, respectively, initiated missionary activities in present-day Georgia and Virginia; and Blessed Diego de Luis de San Vitores, SJ (1627–72), on the island of Guam.

9. HISPANICS HAVE THE LARGEST PERCENTAGE OF LAY CATHOLICS IN FAITH FORMATION AND PASTORAL LEADERSHIP PROGRAMS.

The greatest limitation for Hispanic communities today is the scarce number of Hispanic priests. Indeed, Hispanics are underrepresented in every category of ministry leadership and formation except one: they are overrepresented among lay leaders currently enrolled in formation programs. While permanent deacons and their wives, lay ecclesial ministers, women religious, and non-Hispanic priests provide vital leadership—and fostering such religious vocations remains imperative—grassroots Hispanic Catholic lay leaders are the most abundant resource for Hispanic ministry. They do the bulk of everyday ministry as catechists, youth leaders, prayer group leaders, fundraisers, community organizers, spiritual advisors, translators, immigrant advocates, and much more. Providing personnel and funding for the formation of these lay Hispanic leaders is a crucial challenge in dioceses and parishes across the country.

Another challenge is to help Hispanics who complete diocesan formation programs transition to parish and diocesan leadership responsibilities, and even develop pathways for them to embrace other vocations such as lay ecclesial minister or permanent deacon. The witness of lay Catholics can often revitalize the practice of the faith among their peers even more effectively than the teaching of a priest, deacon, or professional lay minister. Whether in sacramental preparation, evangelization groups, apostolic movements, small faith communities, youth ministries, Catholic schools, and more, pastors and other church personnel today have a magnificent opportunity to engage Hispanic lay leaders who are a prime force for advancing the Catholic faith in our parish communities and in the ordinary circumstances of U.S. daily life.

10. THE HISPANIC PRESENCE IS TRANSFORMING PARISH LIFE.

The involvement and the sheer number of Hispanics are important factors in what is nothing less than a historic shift in the central institution of U.S. Catholic life: the parish. A century ago, when European immigration had transformed the Catholic Church in the United States, numerous national parishes catered to a particular language or cultural group. Today, due to the decreasing number of priests, financial constraints, and growing ethnic diversity, an increasing number of U.S. parishes—nearly 40 percent of them—have significant groups of parishioners from at least two language or cultural groups. Hispanics are a major force in the ongoing evolution of the U.S. Catholic parish from the ethnic enclave to the shared or multicultural congregation.

Unfortunately, the different groups in a parish often coexist in isolation or even in conflict. One woman began to feel "my church isn't my church anymore" when the number of Spanish-speaking parishioners increased. Still, a pitfall to be avoided in addressing such concerns is equating unity with uniformity. In retrospect the incorporation of European-descent Catholics into English-speaking parishes over three generations was prudent, even though most were initially "segregated" in national parishes. Their gradual integration allowed both for the practice of their Catholic faith and for ethnic unity among Europeans to emerge in U.S. parishes. Today the expectation that Hispanics, even recent immigrants, participate primarily or even exclusively in English-language Masses for the sake of "unity" frequently provides a superficial harmony at best. In many cases it causes frustration, resentment, and Hispanics' choice to vote with their feet and abandon participation in Catholic parish life.

We need to learn that building unity within a diverse congregation is not merely a matter of tolerance or "celebrating differences," as is often imagined. Frequently at stake are the issues of how decisions are made and by whom. Intentionally or not, even many parish leaders who welcome their Hispanic sisters and brothers communicate the message that Hispanics are the guests in the house and that Euro-American Catholics are the owners. While hospitality to newcomers is an essential first step, established parishioners must go beyond receiving others in "our" parish to welcoming them home to their own church. The experience of Hispanic and other newcomers throughout the long saga of U.S. Catholicism underscores that God's house is not holy just because all are welcome. God's house is holy because all belong as valued members of the household.

6

Ten Ways Hispanics Are Redefining American Catholicism

Hosffman Ospino

The Immigrant City. This is how many know Lawrence, Massachusetts, a town in New England with a population of about eighty thousand. Perhaps the most appropriate name for Lawrence is The Catholic Immigrant City. Not long ago, it had fifteen Catholic churches, none of which was established to serve Hispanics. Today, the three Catholic parishes left celebrate several Masses in Spanish every week. The transformation took place in about fifty years.

In the Northeast and Midwest, changes like this are more recent. In the South and West, entire generations of Catholics have not known a time without a Hispanic neighbor, the ever-present image of Our Lady of Guadalupe, *quinceañera* celebrations, Masses in Spanish, and some good *empanadas* after worship! What used to be a phenomenon restricted to places like Los Angeles, San Diego, Brownsville, Houston, or Miami is becoming the new norm.

As a researcher of U.S. Catholicism, with particular focus on the Hispanic Catholic experience, I get to meet incredible people in faith communities across the country: tireless pastoral leaders, families passing the faith on to their children in different languages, young people discerning how to integrate the gospel in their lives, immigrants searching for a new life with the same longings as their sisters and brothers who have been in the country a little longer. And they all love being Catholic.

This is not the first time that U.S. Catholicism has been drastically transformed. The arrival of millions of European immigrants in this country in the nineteenth and twentieth centuries had a similar effect. Today's immigrant Catholics are arriving from the global south. Catholics of all cultural backgrounds find themselves sharing their churches with fellow parishioners about whom they know little. Rapid demographic changes along with the fear of the unknown seem to explain some of the anxiety that invades the hearts of many Catholics in the United States today.

The best remedy to address such anxiety is to know more about each other. To that end, here are ten ways Hispanics are redefining American Catholicism in the twenty-first century—and why this is good news for all.

1. HISPANICS ARE AT THE HEART OF THE CHURCH'S GROWTH.

In 1965, there were 48.5 million Catholics in the country. Half a century later the number had risen to about seventy million. Despite millions of baptized women and men who stopped self-identifying as Catholic, the number of Catholics in the United States is growing.

Hispanics account for 71 percent of the growth of the Catholic population in the United States since 1960. Long before 1776, the first Catholics in what is now U.S. territory were Hispanic. They became part of the country as the nation expanded its borders (e.g., Mexican Americans in 1848 and Puerto Ricans in 1898).

Over the last half-century, the growth of the Hispanic population has come through sustained migration patterns from Latin America and the Spanish-speaking Caribbean, including significant numbers of exiles and refugees; high birth rates among Hispanic women, especially immigrants; and family reunification policies.

2. HISPANICS ARE FORMING A NEW GEOGRAPHIC CENTER FOR U.S. CATHOLICISM.

The vast majority of Catholics who arrived from Europe during the nineteenth century and the first half of the twentieth settled mainly in two regions: The Northeast and the Midwest. There these immigrants and their descendants built thousands of parishes, established the largest network of private schools, and founded hundreds of universities. They also built a large network of social services, rivaled in resources and outreach only by the U.S. government. Thanks to this structural presence, Catholics became not only the largest church in the country, but also one of the most influential.

About 61 percent of parishes, 61 percent of Catholic schools, 83 percent of Catholic colleges and universities, 60 percent of seminaries and houses of formation, more than half of Catholic hospitals, and most Catholic publishing companies are located in the Northeast and the Midwest. More than 50 percent of archdioceses and most U.S. cardinals heading a diocese are also in these two regions.

But during the second decade of the twenty-first century, a major threshold was crossed: the majority of U.S. Catholics now live in the South and the West. Hispanics are the major reason for this geographical shift, joined in these regions by the fast-growing Asian population.

It is imperative for the church to build parishes, schools, universities, pastoral institutes, and seminaries and houses of formation in the Southwest. This is a time for Catholic pioneers and entrepreneurs, a time for true missionary work that sets the foundations for what most likely will be growing centers of Catholic life in the United States.

3. HISPANICS ARE TRANSFORMING HOW WE COMMUNICATE WITH EACH OTHER.

There are twenty million immigrants from Latin America and the Spanish-speaking Caribbean presently living in the United States mainland. About fourteen million (60 percent) Hispanic immigrants self-identify as Catholic. If these Catholics constituted one nation, the population would be larger than that of every island in the Caribbean and larger than that of most countries in Latin America.

These demographic comparisons help us assess whether we are investing enough in welcoming and embracing a population that is transforming thousands of Catholic communities in the United States. How much do we understand the lives and practice of the faith of Spanish-speaking Catholics? Do we integrate that knowledge as part of our pastoral planning and outreach?

According to the National Study of Catholic Parishes with Hispanic Ministry (for which I served as the principal investigator), there are about 4,500 parishes in the country with explicit outreach efforts to Hispanics Catholics, primarily in Spanish. Most dioceses and parishes in the country define Hispanic ministry mainly as ministry in Spanish with a focus on immigrant populations.

Hispanic immigrants come from every Spanish-speaking nation in the continent. They bring a rich array of cultural and religious traditions that are redefining the American Catholic experience in the twenty-first century. Thanks to Hispanics, in many parts of the country U.S. Catholicism is a de facto bilingual (or multilingual) reality.

4. TWO-THIRDS OF HISPANIC CATHOLICS IN THE UNITED STATES WERE BORN HERE.

Some pastoral leaders, and many Catholics in the pews, are bewildered to learn that nearly two-thirds of Hispanics are U.S. born (about 65.5 percent). But it should not be a surprise, given that Hispanics are the oldest Catholic group in the land and their growth has been steady for more than a century.

About half of U.S.-born Hispanics self-identify as Catholic. Their lives unfold in a constant process of negotiating identities as both Americans and Hispanics. This both/and experience allows U.S.-born Hispanic Catholics to draw from the riches of multiple cultural wells. That same experience also places them at odds with a society that often sees diversity as a threat—as in the case of negative attitudes toward bilingualism and biculturalism. Hispanics are expected to assimilate quietly into the mainstream.

It is naive to assume that the pastoral needs and faith expressions of U.S.-born Hispanic Catholics are the same as their immigrant relatives. These Hispanics, upon whom much of the future of U.S. Catholicism rests, are forging a new way of being Catholic.

5. A MAJORITY OF U.S. CATHOLICS UNDER 18 ARE HISPANIC.

The median age for Hispanics is twenty-nine, significantly younger than White (forty-three), Asian (thirty-six), and Black (thirty-three) populations. About half of Hispanics are younger than thirty. How are Catholic pastoral leaders reaching out to youth and young adult Hispanic Catholics?

About 60 percent of all U.S. Catholics younger than eighteen are Hispanic. Of that population, 94 percent were born in the United States. Most young Hispanics remain significantly influenced by their immigrant families, retaining their faith, culture, and language. (More than half of all U.S.-born Hispanics above the age of five—about twenty million—speak Spanish at home.)

Although most are English-speaking and grow up embracing many of the values of the larger U.S. culture, they are also influenced by the Spanish language and a faith mediated through Hispanic cultural narratives and symbols. Programs of youth ministry and religious education serving young Hispanics must engage the family. It is important that pastoral leaders affirm—in the most appropriate language—the faith and the role of Hispanic relatives in the process of passing on the faith.

About half of all Catholic millennials are Hispanic. They are choosing careers, deciding on family life, and reevaluating their faith. They question how much to draw from their Hispanic background when integrating into the larger U.S. cultural matrix. Whether the gospel and the best of the Catholic tradition will inform these decisions will largely depend on adequate pastoral accompaniment.

6. ABOUT ONE IN FOUR HISPANICS ARE FORMER CATHOLICS.

The engagement of Hispanic youth and young adult Catholics may be the single most significant factor that will determine the vitality of Catholic communities and pastoral efforts during the next thirty years. These are the young women and men who soon will be sustaining parishes, sending their children to Catholic schools and universities, and leading church ministries.

Yet it is estimated that about a quarter of Hispanics are former Catholics. That is almost fourteen million people who could have been in our communities partaking of the sacraments and discerning ways to better live the gospel. Most of them (about 70 percent) made the decision to "leave the church" before the age of twenty-four. When surveyed, the following are the top two reasons they provided for leaving: they "drifted away" and they "stopped believing in the teachings of their childhood religion." These reasons are similar to those provided by former non-Hispanic young Catholics. Most are joining the ranks of the nonreligiously affiliated (i.e., "nones").

This is a clear indictment of how inadequately we welcome and create spaces for people to fall in love with Jesus Christ and the mysteries of the Christian faith. This is not "normal." Silence in the face of this trend cannot be an option.

7. HISPANICS ARE UNDERREPRESENTED IN CATHOLIC EDUCATION.

By the middle of the twentieth century, more than five million school-age Catholic children (more than 50 percent of this sector of the Catholic population) were enrolled in Catholic schools. Many went to college and then on to successful professional lives. Many became priests, vowed religious, and lay ecclesial ministers. Yet over the last fifty years, enrollment in Catholic education has plummeted, and thousands of schools have closed.

Of the approximately 14.5 million school-age Catholic children today, about eight million (or 55 percent) are Hispanic. The majority reside in the southern and western regions of the country, but barely 4 percent of school-age Hispanic Catholic children are enrolled in Catholic schools. Just about 13 percent of the student population in Catholic colleges and universities is Hispanic.

The large number of Hispanic Catholic children and youth can be an opportunity for renewal and creativity among Catholic educational institutions. Hispanics can bring a new spring to Catholic schools, colleges, and universities. To do so, leaders must do four things: intentionally increase enrollment of Hispanic children; ensure welcoming environments; build new schools and universities where Catholicism is growing; and imagine new models to introduce young Hispanic Catholics to the treasures of Catholic education.

8. THERE IS ROOM FOR GROWTH IN THE NUMBER OF HISPANIC MINISTERS IN THE CHURCH.

The areas of ministerial service where Hispanics are growing most steadily are the permanent diaconate and lay ecclesial ministry. There are about 2,500 Hispanic permanent deacons in the country. About 50 percent of lay Catholics enrolled in ministry formation programs are Hispanic, although only 17 percent of them are in degree-granting programs.

It is not far-fetched to anticipate, given demographic trends, that soon most ministerial leaders for the church in this country will have a Hispanic background. Yet the number of U.S.-born Hispanic priests and vowed women and men religious does not match prevailing population trends. About 83 percent of Hispanic priests and more than 90 percent of Hispanic vowed religious women and men are foreign-born.

Are we overlooking the potential of the U.S.-born Hispanic population to assume ministerial leadership? The cultural, linguistic, and even spiritual needs of U.S.-born Hispanics often demand a distinct type of pastoral accompaniment.

A critical and sustained conversation about Hispanic vocations to ministerial life could address various dynamics, including the following: obstacles to vocational discernment among Hispanics; vocational outreach to U.S.-born Hispanics; welcoming practices in seminaries and houses of formation; cultivation of a culture of vocations among Hispanic families and faith communities; and effective pathways from apostolic service, to which all the baptized are called, to the discernment of more specific vocations to ministerial life within the church.

9. HISPANIC CATHOLICS DRAW FROM DEEP U.S. LATINO AND LATIN AMERICAN FOUNDATIONS.

Hispanic Catholics draw from a rich world of pastoral and theological foundations. The language and the vision of the last four Conferences of Latin American Bishops—Medellín (1968), Puebla (1979), Santo Domingo (1992), and Aparecida (2007)—live in the minds and hearts of countless Latin Americans who did missionary work as catechists and pastoral leaders. The language of Pope

Francis's pontificate (e.g., missionary discipleship, small faith communities, a church that goes out, etc.) is almost second nature to Hispanic immigrants involved in evangelizing activities in their countries of origin.

Also, hundreds of thousands of Hispanic immigrants are associated with the Catholic Charismatic Renewal, a movement that originated in the United States. As they find a home in Catholic parishes nationwide, many bring with them a Latin American style of this spirituality that is renewing entire communities. Nearly half of all parishes with Hispanic ministry have a Catholic Charismatic Renewal community.

Various currents of Latin American theological thought also influenced a smaller group of formally educated Latin American immigrants. They learned methodologies for theological reflection that brought the best of the Catholic tradition into dialogue with the social and human sciences and key sociocultural dynamics that shape the lives of Latin Americans.

In turn, U.S. Hispanic Catholics also draw from important sources of theological and pastoral life grounded in reflection of what it means to be Catholic and Hispanic in this country. The Academy of Catholic Hispanic Theologians of the United States is the third largest Catholic theological guild in the United States. For several decades ACHTUS members, committed to doing theology "on the ground," have been advancing substantial theological reflection in close conversation with Hispanic Catholics.

The Encuentros (Encounters) started as national gatherings of Hispanic pastoral leaders advocating for better outreach to Hispanic Catholics. They evolved into full-fledged processes of consultation, reflection, and evangelization. The Encuentros have inspired a renewed awareness about the Hispanic Catholic presence, the development of new structures, commitments to serve this community well, and the development of dynamic models of pastoral life. Most importantly, the Encuentros have been instrumental in fostering new waves of Catholic pastoral leaders.

10. HISPANIC CATHOLICS OFFER INNOVATIVE APPROACHES TO EVANGELIZATION.

The Fifth National Encuentro of Hispanic/Latino Ministry (Fifth Encuentro) was a four-year process of ecclesial reflection, consultation, and evangelization (2017–20).

The process was driven by a well-defined methodology. It started by listening to Hispanic Catholics and others at the grassroots who spent some time meeting other Catholics living on the peripheries of church and society. What was heard was then discussed in prayer and reflection in small faith communities. Then large meetings—also called Encuentros—at the parish, diocesan, regional, and national levels served to distill the wisdom gathered during several months of listening and discernment. Faith communities identified pastoral priorities and commitments. The process provided a superb background for pastoral planning.

More than anything, the Fifth Encuentro was a process of evangelization that aimed at renewing the nearly five thousand parish communities that engaged in it. It sought to involve at least one million Catholics, mostly Hispanic, and identify at least twenty thousand new Hispanic pastoral leaders. Although the initial time frame was four years, the spirit of Encuentro will likely inspire many conversations well into the future.

The process of the Fifth Encuentro focused primarily on the Hispanic Catholic experience, but it was for the entire church in the United States. The model could become a standard for evangelization initiatives across Catholic communities. It drew from the Scriptures and from centuries of missionary and evangelizing wisdom.

The redefinition of American Catholicism in the twenty-first century—driven in great part by the fast-growing Hispanic presence—is a true blessing and opportunity for all. Five centuries ago, Hispanics planted the first seeds of Catholicism in this land. Two centuries ago, European Catholics and their children built a massive presence that continues to permeate much of the religious and social life of our country. Once again, Hispanics, along with Catholics from various other cultural families, find themselves in a unique position to build the foundations of U.S. Catholicism for decades. The ten ways described above that Hispanics are redefining American Catholicism give us a good sense of what is happening, what is possible, where to invest, and how we can accompany this important sector of the Catholic population in the United States.

Part Two

PASTORAL CONTEXTS FOR HISPANIC MINISTRY

7

Building Communion in Culturally Diverse Parishes

Hosffman Ospino

A group of about fifty Catholics of all ages, made up of families and individuals, approached the priest at the end of a Spanish Mass and asked him to stamp what appeared to be passports. They represented a number of countries and spoke several languages. As the priest stamped their papers, he smiled, shook each person's hand, and said, *"Bienvenidos"* ("Welcome"). Onlookers were naturally curious about these newcomers.

Something similar happened at the end of the Mass celebrated in Vietnamese. The priest stamped cards that looked like passports, smiled, shook hands, and said, *"Xin Chào mùng,"* which means "welcome" in Vietnamese. The story was the same at the end of Mass in English with yet a different priest. Cards were stamped, he smiled, shook hands, and said, *"Welcome."* The reaction of those around was the same: curiosity. For four weeks, the three priests stamped cards for people they hadn't previously seen.

Were these Catholics on an intercontinental pilgrimage? No, they're all members of my home church, St. Patrick parish in Lawrence,

Massachusetts. We belong to a community that celebrates our faith in Jesus Christ in three languages grounded in the many cultures that give life to the neighborhood in which the parish is located. The "passports" were cards that included the names of three languages our parishioners speak most commonly to celebrate their faith. Those who procured three stamps could claim a Bible in their preferred language. This is one of the many exercises over the years that the pastoral team at St. Patrick's has developed to increase awareness about the importance of being a culturally diverse parish where everyone who seeks an encounter with God in the Scriptures, the sacraments, and serving others is welcomed.

Although celebrating the Eucharist in a language other than our mother tongue felt like visiting a different country, we all belong to the same parish community.

CULTURALLY DIVERSE PARISHES YESTERDAY AND TODAY

The first Catholics in what today is part of the United States arrived from Spain in the sixteenth century, many decades before the foundation of our nation. Since then, countless Catholic immigrants have settled in this land and established faith communities. Throughout most of its history, Catholicism in the United States has been practiced in parishes. Yet our understanding of the word *parish,* or communities that function like a parish, has evolved, enriching, transforming, and always giving them new life.

During the sixteenth and seventeenth centuries, Catholics established missions mostly in the South and West that functioned as centers of catechesis and worship as well as trade schools. Missions were a place of encounter, though also often conflict, between the immigrant newcomer Spanish Catholics and the natives of the land. During the nineteenth century and first half of the twentieth century, millions of Catholics migrated from Europe. They settled mainly in the Northeast and the Midwest and built more than twenty thousand parishes in every major city within those regions and beyond.

It was common that Catholics from each national group would build their own parish, allowing them to use the language, cultural, and religious traditions that were familiar. These faith communities, which came to be known as national parishes, represented safe spaces where members could acclimate to their new home. As generations passed, their descendants integrated more fully into the whole of society. They embraced English as a common language and learned new ways of being Catholic that didn't always mirror the traditions of their immigrant relatives.

Toward the middle of the twentieth century, a new way of being a Catholic parish began to take shape. Black, Asian, and Hispanic Catholics worshiped in a small number of parishes. Many of these communities were segregated, reflecting the social dynamics in the larger society. However, anti-segregation movements called for Christians of all races and ethnicities to worship together. Catholics helped lead the way. Several bishops and other pastoral leaders prophetically encouraged integrated parishes, though too often in a manner that left Blacks, Latinos, and Asians feeling they were second-class members of the community. One way of doing this was asking different racial and ethnic communities to worship together in the same building. Catholics in the Northeast and the Midwest may recall Mass being celebrated in English "upstairs" in the upper church and in a different language "downstairs" in the lower church.

During the latter half of the twentieth century and the first two decades of the twenty-first, millions of Catholic immigrants came to the United States. Today, immigrants represent about 25 percent of U.S. Catholics. Most originate from Latin America, Asia, and—recently—Africa. Euro-American, English-speaking Catholics now share parishes with Catholics from various language and cultural groups. This is how it is at St. Patrick Parish in Lawrence. Originally built to meet the spiritual needs of Catholic Irish immigrants, St. Patrick has transitioned to a multicultural parish that now serves three language communities and Catholics from more than a dozen countries.

Today, nearly 40 percent of all Catholic parishes in the country are culturally diverse, representing nearly 6,500 parishes. About 69 percent of those serve Hispanic Catholics. Culturally diverse parishes are defined as faith communities that normally celebrate Mass in at least two languages—most in English and another language—and have large concentrations of immigrant Catholics and/or Catholics who self-identify with nonmajority racial/ethnic groups.

WHAT CULTURALLY DIVERSE PARISHES TEACH US ABOUT CATHOLICISM

Millions of Catholics in the United States celebrate their faith and learn to be missionary disciples through their membership in culturally diverse parishes. These communities teach us several important things. Culturally diverse parishes help us to appreciate more intentionally the Catholicity of the church. Every week we proclaim in the Creed that we believe in the church that is "catholic." This important mark of the church reminds us of its universality as well as its call to communion amidst diversity. Being Catholic simultaneously points to what we are and what we're called to be. In culturally diverse parishes, God calls us to experience Catholicity by embracing one another as we are, with what we bring, including our differences.

Culturally diverse parishes are portals into beauty and wonder. Languages and cultures expand our imagination in surprising ways. Diversity is an always-open invitation to let the Holy Spirit move our souls. When we celebrate our faith in these parishes, we're given the opportunity to witness the divine. The beauty of words, even those we don't understand, and artistic and ritual expressions and practices, which may challenge us, all have the power to open us to fresh ways of being in relationship with God and each other.

Living our Catholic faith in a culturally diverse parish invites us to embrace with humility the fact that living in tension is normal. Catholics with unique stories and experiences and distinct ways to discern their relationship with God—all shaped by cultures—converge in richly diverse communities. We must learn to share our worldviews and perspectives with people from backgrounds different from ours. As children of God who are rooted in the truth of the gospel, we must negotiate differences. Perpetuating either/or perspectives, upholding a desire to impose our cultural way of being on others, and maintaining dismissive polarizing attitudes all result in more harm than good.

Living and celebrating our Christian faith with people of other cultures also enables us to learn more about the next generation of Catholic women and men who are transforming the church in our day. We learn about their joys and hopes, their griefs and anxieties, and in heeding the Second Vatican Council, make them our own. For example, we know that about 60 percent of all U.S. Catholics under the age of eighteen are Hispanic. We should ask ourselves: *How can we better accompany these young Catholics in their faith journey?*

FOUR RECOMMENDATIONS TO BUILD COMMUNION IN DIVERSITY

Most U.S. Catholics who worship in culturally diverse parishes can relate to at least one of the following three realities: (1) Their parish, not long ago, was monolingual and monocultural, then quickly became highly diverse as Catholics from various cultural backgrounds were welcomed. (2) As an immigrant or newcomer, the only parish serving their spiritual needs was this culturally diverse parish, usually thanks to a pastoral leader who was intentional about serving Catholics like them. (3) They were looking for a parish that treated multiple cultural and linguistic backgrounds as gifts that enrich the life of the community, not a problem to be solved. These three realities reveal that culturally diverse parishes are communities constituted by baptized women and men on a faith journey longing for communion with God, others, and the created order. We meet in the culturally diverse parishes and walk together drinking from similar wells. We're accountable to one another. The vibrancy of our parishes will depend on how well we embrace our shared diversity.

You have probably heard the expression "unity in diversity." On the surface, it points to a worthwhile goal. The problem is that unity is often reduced to uniformity or homogeneity. To avoid this impasse, we should speak instead of "communion in diversity." The word *communion* draws from the best of our theological tradition. It points to the life of the triune God who is divine communion: Father, Son, and Holy Spirit. It reminds us that the source of communion is our faith in the risen Lord Jesus Christ and that the church can only achieve that communion as a fruit of the work of the Holy Spirit among us.

Here are four practical ways to build communion in culturally diverse parishes:

1. *Pray and worship together.* Start with the Eucharist, the source and summit of the Christian life. Pray and worship in the languages of your community.

2. *Learn people's stories.* Sometimes we do not trust each other because we do not know who we are. We fear the unknown and retreat from it. Create spaces for all to share their individual story. Listening to each other's stories with interest and respect builds community.

3. *Serve one another.* Identify the most urgent needs of members in your parish and tend to them as a community of believers. Culturally diverse parishes are excellent places to practice Christian solidarity.

4. *Proclaim the good news to one another with joy in the many languages of the community.* Do it incessantly. Remember that the church exists to evangelize, not to assimilate anyone into a particular culture. Share with people in your community the story of God's love in the words that people understand and cherish.

At St. Patrick Parish, we do this on a regular basis. We are not a perfect community, of course, but we give ourselves the chance to embrace and relish in cultural diversity, the chance to see it as a gift from God in the here and now of our shared faith journey.

THE NEED FOR BRIDGE PEOPLE

Every culturally diverse parish needs *bridge people*. Not just bridge builders, although these are also important. Bridge people are women and men grounded in the best of their Christian faith who embody in their words and actions the commitment to communion in diversity. They are inspired by the example of Jesus Christ, the bridge par excellence between heaven and earth, humanity and divinity. Bridge people mediate across cultural variables and bring people together to honor their uniqueness. Bridge people are cultural brokers who open closed doors, clarify confusion, heal wounds, call for a pause when things get difficult, and point the way forward with their example when the community is ready to take the next step. Every cultural community is a seedbed of bridge people.

Bridge people can be pastoral leaders, catechists, volunteers. Anyone in a position of pastoral leadership should embrace that commitment. Yet every Catholic person in these communities needs to be a bridge. The responsibility of building community is everyone's, and we all have much to contribute from our own cultural location.

There is not a standard model for being a bridge person. God calls people with certain strengths at the right time and in the right place. It is a vocation, hence the importance of personal and communal discernment. Having met countless bridge people, I'd like to share three common characteristics I see:

- They excel in their humanity, being true witnesses of the Golden Rule: "In everything do to others as you would have them do to you" (Matt 7:12).
- They're in love with their faith and intentionally try to live authentic Christian lives every moment.
- They exhibit intercultural competence, meaning they communicate, relate, and work well across cultural boundaries.

One of my favorite psalms says, "Unless the LORD builds the house, / those who build it labor in vain" (Ps 127:1). God is our guide. This is where we start, trusting that God walks with us. Nonetheless, building communion in a culturally diverse parish can't happen in a vacuum. We must listen to one another and understand well the context in which we live and practice our faith. This can happen only with the commitment of people of faith who understand the value of being a parish and the importance of welcoming everyone who seeks the love of God.

8

Parish Celebrations of Our Lady of Guadalupe

Timothy Matovina

One of the most memorable Guadalupe liturgies in which I participated was the *serenata* (serenade) celebrated on the eve of her
December 12 feast at San Antonio's San Fernando Cathedral. The fes-
tivity and fervor of the event inundated the senses—bright colors,
the aroma of fresh flowers, the excitement of the crowd, and the
service of emotive singing. But the most impressive moment was
the reenactment of Guadalupe's apparitions to Saint Juan Diego.
True to this foundational narrative of Mexican and Mexican American faith, the first bishop of Mexico, Juan de Zumárraga, was por-
trayed as skeptical when he first heard Juan Diego's message that
Guadalupe wanted a temple built in her honor. The scoffing of the
bishop's assistants elicited agonizing winces from some onlookers,
stony silence from others. As the story unfolds, the bishop comes to
believe when the stooped *indio* stands erect, drops out-of-season
roses from his *tilma* (cloak), and presents the image of Guadalupe
that miraculously appeared on the *tilma*. As the repentant bishop
and his assistants fell to their knees in veneration, applause erupted
throughout the cathedral.

Such dramatic reenactments of Juan Diego's encounters with Our Lady of Guadalupe are one of the most common ritual practices at parish celebrations of her feast. Thus, liturgical and other parish leaders would do well to familiarize themselves with the *Nican Mopohua* (a title derived from the document's first words, "here is recounted"), the Nahuatl-language apparitions account that devotees acclaim as the foundational text of the Guadalupe tradition.

As translated in Virgilio Elizondo's book *Guadalupe: Mother of the New Creation*, the text narrates Juan Diego's tender encounters with Guadalupe, whose first words to him were "dignified Juan, dignified Juan Diego." She sent him to request that Bishop Zumárraga build a temple at Tepeyac (in present-day Mexico City), where she "will show and give to all people all my love, my compassion, my help, and my protection." In one of the most moving passages of the narrative, Juan Diego returned to her from an unsuccessful interview with the bishop and asked that she send another messenger "who is respected and esteemed" because he deemed himself too unworthy. Her response was tender but firm: "Know well in your heart that there are not a few of my servants and messengers to whom I could give the mandate of taking my thought and my word so that my will may be accomplished. But it is absolutely necessary that you personally go and speak about this, and that precisely through your mediation and help, my wish and my desire be realized." Her words to Juan Diego when he was troubled about the illness of his uncle, Juan Bernardino, are the most quoted among contemporary devotees: "Do not let your countenance and heart be troubled; do not fear that sickness or any other sickness or anxiety. Am I not here, your mother?"

GUADALUPE AND HER FAITHFUL

Celebrating the story of Guadalupe's maternal care and Juan Diego's struggle and exultation does not obliterate the painful daily realities of numerous devotees. Many have stinging memories of the polite disdain or outright hostility they have met in their dealings with salesclerks, bosses, coworkers, teachers, police officers, healthcare providers, social workers, government employees, professional colleagues, and even religious leaders. Thus, it is not surprising that they resonate with the ritual enactment of Juan Diego's rejection, his election as an unexpected hero, his unwavering faith, and his final vindication. Numerous devotees attest that Guadalupe uplifts them as she did Juan Diego, strengthening them in their trials and difficulties. In a word, they confess that the Guadalupe narrative is true: it reveals the deep truth of their human dignity and exposes the lie of experiences that diminish their fundamental sense of worth.

Theological writings about Guadalupe spanning more than three and a half centuries are consistent with this intuition of the faithful. Strikingly, from the first published theological work on Guadalupe, Miguel Sánchez's influential 1648 book, *Imagen de la Virgen María*, down to the present, those who have explored the theological meaning of Guadalupe have not focused primarily on typical Marian topics, such as her title *Theotokos* ("God bearer," or Mother of God), perpetual virginity, Immaculate Conception, and Assumption. Rather, theologians have examined the Guadalupe image, apparitions account, and its historical context as a means to explore the collision of civilizations between the Old and the New Worlds and the ongoing implications of this clash for Christianity in the Americas and beyond.

Today, Guadalupe is most frequently associated with both the struggle to overcome the negative effects of the conquest of the Americas and the hope for a new future of greater justice, faith, and evangelization. Theologies of Guadalupe are thus an ongoing effort to articulate a Christian response to one of the most momentous events of Christianity's second millennium: the conquest, evangelization, and struggles for life, dignity, and self-determination of the peoples of the Americas.

Understanding Guadalupe within this broad context is crucial for those who prepare celebrations of her feast. Also essential is appreciating how this context shapes the depths of what she means to her faithful daughters and sons. In her study of Guadalupe in the lives of Mexican American women, Jeanette Rodriguez reports that when she asked an indigenous woman in Mexico what makes Guadalupe different from other images of Mary, the woman simply responded, *Se quedó* (She stayed).

Like this woman, numerous devotees are attracted to Guadalupe because they see someone who has ever been with them and with their people. They see a mother who will never let them down and to whom they can freely pour out their hearts' concerns. What matters most is not that their prayers are always answered in the manner desired, but that they see in Guadalupe's face someone who cares about them, someone who is ever willing to listen. In a word, what they see in Guadalupe's face is faithfulness, a mother and a presence that never abandons them.

For many, the core experience of Guadalupe is the replication of Juan Diego's intimate, mystical encounter with their celestial mother. In innumerable conversations, prayers, and sustained gazes at her image, devotees relive this mystical encounter. Thus, one of the most important preparations for a parish Guadalupe feast is to establish an attractive space where devotees can approach their celestial mother. A common practice is to have a procession—often at the conclusion of the Eucharist—during which congregants present roses to Guadalupe with their prayers.

Yet, and perhaps somewhat ironically, Guadalupe's constant protection of her people presents one of the greatest challenges for celebrations in her honor. Some pastors have bemoaned that Guadalupan and other "popular devotions are nothing more than 'a Catholicism of a day'…stressing great but isolated moments of fervor, yet failing to translate into deep and lasting spiritual transformation and sustained participation in the life of the church." One priest with half a century of experience in Hispanic ministry asserted that many devotees seem "locked into" their "attraction to the Virgin [of Guadalupe] as a source of favors" and pay scant attention to living out the discipleship and evangelization church leaders proclaim as Guadalupe's call to her devotees.

Such statements accentuate the most enduring pastoral challenge of Guadalupan veneration and feast-day celebrations: devotees' tendency to focus on the favors Guadalupe bestows rather than on the life of discipleship to which she summons her faithful. The first Guadalupan pastoral manual, Luis Laso de la Vega's 1649 work *Huei tlamahuiçoltica*, enumerated various miracles of Guadalupe on behalf of the native peoples and all those who turn to her. But it emphasized even more that the proper response to Guadalupe's maternal care is to live as daughters and sons who express their gratitude by following the commands of her son, Jesus Christ. Laso de la Vega's entreaty that pastoral leaders guide devotees beyond seeking favors to seeking deeper faith commitment is as timely today as ever.

PARISH GUADALUPE CELEBRATIONS

One effective way to address this concern is to help devotees link Guadalupe's feast day with the Advent season in which it falls. The origins of the feast date back to 1754, when Pope Benedict XIV established December 12 as its date on the liturgical calendar. In 1988, leaders of the Instituto Nacional de Liturgia Hispana worked with the Subcommittee on Hispanic Liturgy of the U.S. Bishops' Committee on the Liturgy (now the Committee on Divine Worship) to successfully petition the Vatican to elevate annual Guadalupe liturgical celebrations from the rank of "memorial" to "feast" in the United States. Then at the request of the 1997 Special Assembly for America of the Synod of Bishops, Pope John Paul II declared it an official liturgical feast for all the Americas. Along with the general option of choosing readings from the Common of the Blessed Virgin Mary, for the Guadalupe feast the Lectionary used in the United States has specific options for the gospel and the first reading that are clearly consistent with the Advent theme of joyfully preparing the way for the Lord's coming: the Annunciation (Luke 1:26–38), the Visitation with the first line of the Magnificat (Luke 1:39–47), and Zechariah 2:10–13, which begins "Sing and rejoice, O daughter Zion! See, I am coming to dwell among you, says the Lord."

When the Guadalupe apparitions are dramatically reenacted before Mass or after the Gospel—or even when they are not—the meaning of the apparitions can be interwoven with the Eucharist and the Advent season. For example, various homilists have developed the insight that, just as Mary visited Elizabeth and shared the good news of Christ, so Guadalupe visited Juan Diego—and through him the peoples of America—to bring her maternal love and the good news of her son. This message calls us to live the spirituality of Advent: awaiting in joy the coming of Christ as Mary and her kinswoman Elizabeth did and imitating them in announcing the good news of his coming, just as Our Lady of Guadalupe did to Juan Diego and he in turn did to others.

Guadalupe's call to discipleship can be further accentuated through building a strong relationship between the Eucharist and expressions of Guadalupan devotion. Preachers have sought to link the Eucharist, the assigned Scripture texts for the feast, and the narrative of Guadalupe's encounters with Juan Diego. In one homily, Allan Figueroa Deck, SJ, observed that the relation between Guadalupe and her faithful "is sometimes simply that of a loving mother who literally lavishes care and concern on her needy children." He contended that this is only half the meaning of Guadalupe, because "the story of Tepeyac," like the gospel accounts of the Annunciation and the Visitation, "graphically portrays the central role of love and service in our Christian lives." Exhorting his listeners to put into action their gratitude for the gift of God's love offered in their Mother Guadalupe and in the Eucharist, he concluded, "Seized and saturated by such love, what will be our response to others, especially those most in need?"

Devotional practices present yet another opportunity for proclaiming Guadalupe's call to discipleship. The most widespread communal devotion for the Guadalupe feast is *las mañanitas* (literally, "morning songs"), a tribute usually begun before dawn. In many parishes it leads into the feast-day Mass. Devotees offer flowers to express their love and thanks to their mother. Accompanying the song tributes are devotions such as the praying of the Rosary, Scripture readings, and testimonies or meditations about Guadalupe. Sacred dances are also offered to Guadalupe by groups called *matachines*, sometimes within the Eucharist itself during the entrance procession, the Presentation of the Gifts, or after Communion.

Resounding in the song offerings are sentiments of joyful veneration, such as the beginning and ending of the traditional hymn *Buenos días, Paloma Blanca* (Good Morning, White Dove): *Buenos días, Paloma Blanca, hoy te vengo a saludar....Recibe estas mañanitas, de mi humilde corazón* (Good morning, White Dove, today I come to greet you....Receive these *mañanitas* from my humble heart). Most of Guadalupe's faithful know these songs by heart and resonate with their emphases on thanking her, seeking her blessing and protection, and acclaiming her motherhood, purity, and miraculous apparitions to Juan Diego.

The specific contours of such practices vary from community to community, but in every parish they provide opportunities to creatively engage people's faith expressions. Parish leaders should take care not to merely coopt devotees' traditions, but to respectfully join the people in their veneration, even as they help bring out its deeper significance. Because there is no single order of worship for a *las mañanitas* celebration, pastors and liturgists can help plan prayers, personal faith testimonies, Scripture readings, and/or meditations in a manner that complements the traditional songs. These enhancements should be brief so as to not detract from the song tribute that comprises the core faith expression of this event. But when done well, these additional worship elements help devotees deepen their appreciation of their traditions.

One lay leader, Socorro Durán, presented a moving meditation for *las mañanitas* at her parish. She reminded those struggling with illness, poverty, unemployment, inadequate education, a lack of legal status, insecurity, or any kind of discouragement or difficulty that our times are "not that different" from Mexico at the time of Juan Diego or the time of Jesus over two thousand years ago. In Durán's words, our ancestors of those past days "didn't have many reasons to hope either." But just as Christ's birth and Juan Diego's encounter with Guadalupe were both "a sudden, unexpected event which then and now brings hope and expectation to us," so too the Guadalupe feast "renews hope in our wilting spirits" and enables us to be instruments of Christ and our Mother Guadalupe for a world in need of healing.

Some parishes enact bilingual celebrations to extend Guadalupe's evangelizing message to non-Latinos and to Latinos, especially the young who are not proficient in Spanish. Opting for such a celebration must be done with careful pastoral discernment, lest devotees be left with the sense that their traditional feast has been taken from them. Hispanic leaders should be fully involved in any such decision-making process. An approach that suits some parish contexts is to conduct a service like *las mañanitas* in Spanish and then celebrate a bilingual Eucharist, with Spanish as the primary language as the situation warrants.

In worship communities where leaders decide on a bilingual celebration of the Eucharist, the usual guidelines for such celebrations apply. First and foremost, as Mark Francis, CSV, has noted, the primary purpose of such liturgies is "not to celebrate cultural diversity" but "to help each member of the assembly participate fully, actively and consciously in the liturgy." Recommendations to enact this vision include making the words of the prayers and Scripture readings accessible to as many as possible; avoiding excessive translated duplication of spoken words through skillful use of language and printed worship aids; and paying attention to nonverbal communications such as art, environment, symbol, gesture, and prayerful silence. Pastoral musicians who form bilingual choirs can also greatly enliven such celebrations, provided they make sure to highlight some of the traditional hymns many devotees sing with full voice on their Mother Guadalupe's feast.

One of the most difficult challenges for parish liturgy occurs in years when December 12 falls on a Sunday. Of course, Catholic liturgical norms state that Sunday Mass has precedence over feast days, in this case the Mass for the Third Sunday of Advent. Some pastors have allowed a feast-day Mass on the Sunday. Others have made a compromise decision of a celebration that is either subsumed into the Sunday Advent liturgy or does not interfere with the regular Sunday Mass schedule, either an alternative Sunday Mass time or celebrating on a day other than Sunday. Whatever approach is used, pastors and liturgical coordinators should address this concern well in advance and involve Hispanic parish leaders in their deliberations. Whatever the final decision, in communities with fervent Guadalupan devotees, it is pastorally desirable to find some way to worthily celebrate the Guadalupe feast.

A FEAST FOR ALL

While Guadalupan devotion is most conspicuous among Mexicans and Mexican Americans, the Guadalupe feast is for all. Two-thirds of Hispanics in the United States are of Mexican heritage, but pastoral leaders from other Hispanic groups such as Colombian émigré Fanny Tabares remind us about the need to address intra-Hispanic relations in ethnically mixed Latino communities. Tabares notes that South Americans in the United States are "a minority group within the Hispanic community" who make great sacrifices to "accept as their own customs which, though Hispanic, originated in countries not their own."

Many participate in the religious traditions of other Hispanic groups, especially the predominant Guadalupe feast, and can be chagrined at the comparatively tepid appreciation for Catholic feasts from their own countries of origin. Every country in Latin America and the Caribbean has a national Marian patroness. Particularly in worship communities that encompass diverse Hispanic groups, recognition of this diversity of Marian traditions through creative Marian litanies, other prayers, or allusions in homilies can help unite diverse Hispanic communities in their celebration of the Guadalupe feast.

Moreover, non-Latino Catholics increasingly embrace Guadalupan devotion. St. Mark the Evangelist parish in San Antonio is one of a growing number of primarily Euro-American parishes that prominently celebrate the Guadalupe feast. Within a few years of beginning this annual celebration, the parish Guadalupana devotional society grew from twelve mostly Hispanic members to nearly 140, both men and women, nearly half of them European Americans.

Pastoral leaders would do well to encourage trends such as these in parishes with diverse populations.

Guadalupe is a source of collective pride for Mexicans and Mexican Americans, and she has enabled many to deepen their faith and sense of human dignity. Yet those very devotees are often the first to acclaim Guadalupe as a mother whose care extends to all her children from every background. Liturgies for the Guadalupe feast in U.S. parishes present a vital pastoral opportunity to help write the next chapter in the history of the Guadalupe tradition, one in which her stated intent to "show and give to all people all my love, my compassion, my help, and my protection" can be more fully realized.

9

Apostolic Movements

Timothy Matovina

Elisabeth Román was raised in a strict Pentecostal household and told from an early age about the evils of Catholicism. Faced with a personal crisis and lacking a spiritual home after a twenty-year hiatus from church attendance, she accepted a friend's invitation to a parish Mass imbued with the spirit of the Catholic Charismatic Renewal. Elisabeth continued to worship at the Charismatic Mass. Impressed with the community's faith, her own sense of inner peace, and the fact that no one pressured her to become Catholic, she decided to be received into the Catholic Church. She is convinced that "for Hispanics, who must live between two cultures, charismatic Catholicism can offer the best of both worlds: participation in the sacraments and a personal, livelier form of worship, which is at the heart of our religious experience."

The witness of Elisabeth Román reveals the potential of apostolic movements in Hispanic communities. Hispanics have long participated in pious societies such as the Hijas de María, Catholic Action, and the Guadalupanas. These organizations promote the worthy reception of the sacraments, devotional practice, and a life of faith and virtue.

Today, the needs of Hispanic communities are more urgent than ever. Many confront problems such as a lack of opportunity for employment and education, low educational attainment, drug and alcohol abuse, violence, teenage pregnancy, poverty, undocumented status, xenophobic and racist oppression, inadequate healthcare, and a general strain on family cohesion and personal well-being, among others. Looking inward to the vitality of their own faith communities, Hispanic ministry leaders have frequently lamented that the upsurge of religious traditions like Pentecostalism and evangelicalism provide the most momentous challenge. Many Protestants criticize Catholic practices such as holy images or the veneration of Mary. They often go door-to-door, trying to convince Catholics to change religions. Transmitting the faith to children, grandchildren, and other young people is more challenging than ever.

In the midst of this situation, apostolic movements have emerged to form Catholics in faith, the life of prayer, relations with the Holy Spirit, and evangelization. Most importantly, these movements promote not just a cultural Catholicism, but a Catholicism of commitment. Today, one of the great challenges and opportunities for Hispanic ministry is to guide the leaders of the apostolic movements in their ministries of formation and evangelization. Let us examine the primary pastoral challenges and opportunities that these movements present for Hispanic ministry.

PASTORAL CHALLENGES

Spiritual Elitism: Unfortunately, there is a tendency in some apostolic movements to consider their group the best way, or even the only way, to follow Jesus. I remember the first youth retreats in which I participated as a teenager. The movement was called Search. When I met people who had other spiritual experiences, I would think, "This is good, but you need to live the Search retreat to truly deepen your friendship with Christ." At that time, I was not conscious of a fundamental truth: there are many roads to Christ and what matters most is to know and serve him in the way that God ordains for each one of us. Feeling I was superior to others because of the apostolic movement to which I belonged was a mistake and, in some instances, distanced me from the very persons I wanted to invite to the Search retreats.

Competitive Spirit: This is similar to spiritual elitism. Sometimes there is a competitive spirit between leaders of different movements or groups. We give the impression that we don't even profess the same Catholic faith! When we begin to speak of "my group," something is not right. The goal is not to elevate "my" group over other leaders and "their" groups. All groups should work together for the cause of Christ. As Jesus said, "The greatest among you will be your servant" (Matt 23:11). Invite and evangelize, yes, but never compete with my sisters and brothers who serve the same God and share the same Catholic faith.

Problems with Authority: Perhaps this is the greatest challenge. As leaders we should obey the inspirations of the Holy Spirit, but sometimes we act as if the Spirit only speaks to us. I remember a man from a prayer group. He had a profound spiritual experience and wanted to completely change his life. Just a few weeks after his conversion, when he heard a testimony about missions, he announced that God had put in his heart a call to preach in Africa. The fact that he had four small children and had not consulted with his wife did not seem to him like relevant factors for his discernment. No, he had a direct revelation from God, and there was no authority that could convince him otherwise.

Although this is an extreme case, sometimes we are like this man: we do not want to listen to the voice of God in the guidance and authority of others. Even the regional and national coordinators of the Catholic Charismatic Renewal say that some prayer group leaders do not heed the counsel of those who seek to support them with their more ample experience. Sometimes apostolic groups conduct their own formation classes in such a manner that neither parish nor diocesan leaders influence the members of their group. It could be that their group formation classes are good and even necessary, but we should be attentive to the tendency to trust solely in our own judgement and authority. We need to animate apostolic movement leaders to participate in diocesan and parish formation programs so they can continue to grow in spiritual maturity and pastoral wisdom.

Forgetting the Necessities of the Parish: One of the most frequent complaints about apostolic movements from pastors is that the participants are so busy with the activities of their group that they don't have time for the parish. One pastor I met did not want the *Cursillo* movement in his parish because another priest had told him that, as the movement grew, the commitment of the people to the needs of the parish would diminish. Of course, pastors should respect and even encourage the evangelizing potential of the apostolic movements. At the same time, however, members of the movements should seek ways to be a leaven in the parish. This balance between participating in a group and supporting the mission of the whole parish—with time, talents, and monetary donations—is one of the most important pastoral challenges that the apostolic movements face.

Seeking Spiritual Consolation Rather than a Faith of Commitment: Here we see a very subtle temptation. Frequently, experiences of God touch us profoundly. We openly confess our faults and failings. We encounter a deep peace. We embrace our sisters and brothers in Christ. We bathe ourselves in tears of repentance. We dance and shout with joy. We feel the magnificent presence of God. All of this can be very good.

Yet we must remember that sentiments are a way to encounter God, but they are not God. The principal fruit of an encounter with God is not what we feel; it is the transformation of our life. Many people confuse this point. In the worst cases, when they no longer feel the same fervor within their group, they think that now there is no reason to continue living their faith. Confusing what I feel with the commitment and determination to change my life is a great temptation. We need to remind people who participate in apostolic movements that spiritual consolations are a gift that God gives us that urge us along on the pathway to conversion.

Focus Solely on Prayer, Neglecting to Work for Justice: How many times have I heard a person dedicated to prayer criticize those who struggle in God's name for justice! It is important to begin with prayer and conform our efforts to God's will, but it is not right to say that "spiritual" persons do not get involved in practical ways in the problems of the community because to do so is "pure politics." Obviously, I am not speaking of partisan politics nor of demanding that Catholics vote for a designated candidate. I am speaking of moral issues such as abortion, racism, immigration, and the education of our children. For these issues, the voice of a Christian should proclaim justice as did the prophets in the history of salvation, from Isaiah to Jesus himself.

Thanks be to God, apostolic movements are growing in their consciousness of the need to struggle for justice, for example, in their increasing efforts to defend the rights and humanity of immigrants. It is not right to separate prayer from the struggle for justice. As Saint Augustine said, we should pray as if all depended on God, and act as if it all depended on us. And as Pope Francis instructs us, prayer incites us to be the voice, the hands, and the feet of Jesus in the world.

PASTORAL OPPORTUNITIES

The pastoral opportunities that apostolic movements present for Hispanic ministry complement—and I contend they outweigh—the pastoral challenges. Let's examine some of these opportunities.

Renewing Our Faith: I am always impressed with the response of the people when I am invited to give presentations for formation events. Hispanics sacrifice greatly to participate in these events: they travel large distances after a long week of work, even when they must bring their small children with them, and they do it with joy and enthusiasm to learn and grow in their faith! Their hunger to know the Bible and the teachings of our faith are an immense gift God has put in their hearts.

Many youth groups, Bible studies, and prayer groups are an effective response to this hunger. The opportunity to share and deepen our faith in these groups is enormous and highly necessary. More and more groups focus not only on the Bible, but also on other topics, such as the teachings of the popes, Catholic social teaching, the rosary and Marian piety, other devotions like the adoration of the Blessed Sacrament, and many other treasures of our Catholic faith.

Apostolic movements become schools of faith for numerous Catholics. We need to value and enhance these schools.

Attract Persons to the Reception of the Sacraments: I remember very well the way the retreatants received the sacrament of reconciliation the first time I went on a *Cursillo.* Seeing the joy in the face of someone whose soul God had cleansed with the grace of forgiveness was one of the most beautiful miracles of the experience. During Search and *Cursillo* retreats, I too experienced the sacrament of reconciliation at a depth I had never experienced before. The same occurred with our celebrations of the Eucharist and with Holy Hours before the Blessed Sacrament. These were powerful moments of sacramental grace, communion, and fellowship.

For many, the sacraments are the pearl of great price in our church that we least appreciate. However, the apostolic movements offer us opportunities to grow in the grace of the sacraments. Those who receive the sacraments frequently, thanks to the movements, enrich our sacramental life in the parish with their fervent participation in Sunday Eucharist and in the sacrament of reconciliation. All leaders of apostolic movements should promote the sacraments as the great treasure that they are.

Counteract Proselytism: How many of our sisters and brothers have gone over to other religions because they did not know how to respond to questions and criticisms of our Catholic faith? It is true that it is not easy to understand our faith. We need to realize that our faith is so rich and profound that we cannot learn all of it in a single course, not even in a single lifetime, but how sad that our knowledge is at times so poor many of us become confused when we are questioned. We need to learn our faith. We need more groups that are an effective alternative to proselytism. There is a great necessity—and opportunity—to confront this situation with the apostolic movements. They have proven to be a vital means for grassroots Catholics to learn their faith. We should promote and continue to develop their crucial apostolic endeavors.

Healing from Drug and Alcohol Abuse, Personal and Familial Problems: Life conversions are often dramatic among those who get involved in the apostolic movements. Many say they are nothing less than miracles of grace, radical transformations that refashion us into new creations in Christ. The movements and prayer groups are a fertile ground for the work of the Holy Spirit in our lives. The healing is not just of individuals, but also of families. In the same way that the problems of one family member affects the whole family, the renewal of that person's spiritual well-being results in a positive change for all. The curing of souls is one of the most convincing signs the apostolic movements offer that a God full of love and power is present in our world.

Creating a Sense of Belonging: Members of apostolic movements create communities. This has been vital for Hispanics, as many of them have encountered a spiritual family in the movements. Actually, the whole parish family should help create a sense of belonging, but often the joy of belonging begins in the movements. A fundamental necessity of immigrants, those who are far from their families, the divorced, the abandoned, the rejected—ultimately, every human being—is to feel part of a community whose members mutually support and love one another. Apostolic movements are these communities for numerous Hispanics.

Form Leaders as Apostles in Their Daily Lives: Latinos encounter the call to be apostles at the heart of the apostolic movements. The movements prepare apostles to continue the mission of Jesus. They do not accept that their members remain passive Catholics; they inspire them to become active disciples who announce the good news. Many Catholics fail in this regard, but the apostolic movements incite valiant evangelizers who proclaim the gospel in word and in deed: in their homes, their work, the streets, wherever they find themselves in their daily lives.

Form New Leaders for Parishes: Despite the criticism that the movements "rob" leaders from the ministries of the parish, frequently what happens is precisely the opposite. In many places, parish ministries—be they with liturgy, youth, catechesis, or social action—are in the hands of those who have been formed in apostolic movements. Often their fervor is contagious with other parishioners. I recall one woman who, after deepening her relationship with Christ in a prayer group, began to serve as a lector at Sunday Mass. When she proclaimed the Scriptures, her face and her voice radiated her love of the Word of God. The movements should always urge their members to participate in parish ministries with such devotion and humility. In this way the parish is converted into a community of communities, a household of faith where the movements are a school of formation that, like leaven, makes the "dough" of God's grace rise within the hearts of all.

Vocations to the Priesthood, the Diaconate, the Religious Life, and Lay Ecclesial Ministry: The scarcity of priests and religious vocations in Hispanic communities is notable. Thankfully, the number of Hispanics who answer God's call to these vocations is beginning to rise, and the number of Hispanic deacons and their wives who serve in diverse ministries is increasing even more. Many vocations have come from the apostolic movements. As Bishop Daniel Flores of Brownsville, Texas, said, "Without a personal relationship with Jesus Christ, there is no Christian vocation of any kind." In enabling a personal encounter with Christ, the movements inflame the desire to dedicate our lives to God. In this way, they are a wellspring of vocations. Yet the need for vocations continues to increase with the growth of Latinos in the church. The ongoing challenge and opportunity to promote vocations is a priority for every apostolic group.

When apostolic movement leaders work with their pastors and reveal their evangelizing potential, they become one of the most valuable forces to advance faith in the everyday lives of others. The novel *Les Misérables*, by the French author Victor Hugo, offers a good image to illustrate the capacity of the movements to gain souls for Christ. Jean Valjean, the main character, is reviled as a criminal after completing a prison sentence for the simple offense of robbing bread to feed his hungry nephews. He wanders from place to place but cannot find work nor a way to begin his life anew. One day, a bishop receives Valjean into his home and invites him to eat and stay the evening. In his desperation, Valjean takes some valuable pieces of silverware from the cupboard and sneaks away into the night. A police officer detains him and triumphantly marches him to the bishop's house to prove his guilt.

But then the unexpected happens. The bishop thanks the official for returning Valjean, explaining that due to his haste, his guest had forgotten to take other valuable items. Left alone with the shame-faced Valjean, the bishop invites him to take all the contents of his cupboard and to use them to begin a new life. He only asks one indulgence in return: that Valjean remember with these material goods the bishop has "bought your soul for God." The rest of *Les Misérables* could be summarized as the pathway of Jean Valjean to sanctity.

In this encounter, the bishop gave Valjean what he himself had received: the passage from sin and death to a new life in Christ. This is the heart of evangelization: to live our faith in such a way that others are attracted to live it as well. As we reflect on the pastoral challenges and opportunities of the apostolic movements, let us pray that we too can know God and draw many others to God's love through our words, actions, and witness.

10

Catechesis and the Bible among Hispanics

Hosffman Ospino

To speak of a catechesis that is essentially unique to the U.S. Latino/a experience with characteristics that are relevant mostly because of the U.S. Latino/a reality poses a twofold challenge: one, it can send religious educators in search of something that may not exist as specifically defined or creatively imagined; two, it may lead to the temptation of isolating, perhaps caricaturizing, catechesis with Latinos/as, the effects of which would be very detrimental. Nonetheless, there are experiences that U.S. Latino/a Catholics share that shape our identity and allow us to ask specific questions about our relationship with God and others in society and the church. These experiences serve as lenses through which U.S. Latinos/as see reality, interpret it, and respond to it. This does not happen outside the larger ecclesial community but firmly rooted in it. U.S. Latino/a Catholicism must neither be construed as a separate or alternative experience of being church nor as something that possesses lesser value when compared to other experiences of being Catholic. The uniqueness of Latino/a Catholicism, and thus of the way catechesis takes place in our communities as well as how we read Sacred Scripture, rests in its profound ecclesiality. When we catechize, we do it as Latinos/as and not only for Latinos/as. When we read Sacred Scripture, we read it as Latinos/as and not only for Latinos/as.

Instead of pursuing the idea of a "Latino/a catechesis" and how the Bible would be used within such a reality, I propose that we look at what can be named "everyday moments of encounter with the sacred" in the experience of Latino/a Catholics in the United States and explore the engagement of the Scriptures within these moments. The sacred here must not be reduced to something otherworldly, radically transcendent, or even contrary to human experience. The sacred is the perceived presence of God in the realm of life, history, and nature. It is what makes possible that women and men see the world as sacramental. Catechesis for many Latinos/as, as well as for many non-Hispanic Catholics, often happens in classrooms and in the context of formal catechetical encounters. However, catechesis is not limited to these moments. The more aware we are about the everyday moments of encounter with the sacred that characterize the religious experience of U.S. Latino/a Catholics and the more we stress their catechetical value, the better we will be able to appreciate their potential to mediate people's experience of God. These moments simultaneously reveal an initial appropriation of Sacred Scripture and the yearning for a more profound engagement of the sacred text and its message.

LITURGICAL AND PRAYER MOMENTS

Perhaps the most regular encounter with the Scriptures for many Latino/a Catholics is the Word of God proclaimed in the various liturgical celebrations of the church, more particularly in the Eucharist. There, the faithful are nourished from "the table both of God's word and of Christ's body," as the Second Vatican Council's Constitution on Divine Revelation, *Dei Verbum*, reminds us (no. 21). By participating in the liturgical celebrations around the sacraments, the faithful have the opportunity to experience Sacred Scripture become life not only in the proclamation but also in the ritual celebration of

God's Word. Thus, participation in the liturgy has a double catecheti-cal effect: we encounter Sacred Scripture through words (proclama-tion) and actions (ritual).

Along with the encounter with Sacred Scripture in the liturgy, the church encourages Catholics to read the Bible as part of our daily spiritual exercises. Indeed, this is a significant development in the recent history of Catholicism considering that only a century ago those who read the Scripture on their own, when they had a copy, were considered somewhat suspect. *Dei Verbum* insists that "easy access to Sacred Scripture should be provided for all the Christian faithful" (no. 22). This proximity to Sacred Scripture becomes truly palpable in the centuries-long practice of *lectio divina*, a simple yet profound approach to the sacred text in prayer that is well known among many Latino/a Catholics in the United States, particularly *los jóvenes* (the young), and continues to be practiced in homes, Bible study groups, and small Christian communities. Through *lectio div-ina* we listen to God's own words addressing our lives, we become familiar with the biblical texts, and we engage Sacred Scripture as a compass that guides our existence in today's world.

FORMAL STUDY OF SCRIPTURES

One of the many blessings of the Catholic experience in the United States is the existence of a large number of educational centers where people can engage in the formal study of Sacred Scripture. Univer-sities, seminaries, schools, diocesan programs, pastoral institutes, parishes, among others, offer various programs of study at different levels that ultimately lead Christians to a more educated understand-ing of the sacred text. In these centers it is encouraging to see that numerous educators and scholars combine efforts to share their best insights to read Sacred Scripture with the ecclesial community and thus equip women and men interested in the Bible to better read the text in light of current scholarship and creative methodologies.

I would like to highlight the amazing role of the various *insti-tutos pastorales* serving Latino/a Catholics throughout the United States. For Latinos/as, these pastoral institutes are true schools of leadership formation rooted in the study of Sacred Scripture. I have been invited to teach in some of them and am familiar with the curriculum of others. Nearly all of them provide solid introductory programs to Sacred Scripture. The number of Hispanic Catholics who attend these pastoral institutes is significantly larger than those who attend universities and seminaries. Thus, all recognition, support, and accompaniment ought to be given to these institutes committed to faith formation of Latino/a Catholics. They are indeed unique centers of encounter with the Bible.

In some sense, these first two everyday moments of encounter with the sacred are very familiar to Latino/a Catholics and religious educators. We could say that they are more regular, formal, and even "official." Let us now turn to three other moments of encounter with the sacred where Latinos/as engage Sacred Scripture in profound and transformative ways. These perhaps do not enjoy the formality or the recognition of the first two, yet they significantly shape the religious experience of millions of Latino/a Catholics in the United States.

LIVED EXPERIENCE

Lived experience is the unfolding of human life in the context of *lo cotidiano*, the everyday. Latino/a theologians and faith educators concur with the observation that lived experience is perhaps the most powerful catechetical school that we possess. U.S. Latino/a Catholics struggle to fully affirm our identity as Latinos/as, as Catholics, and as citizens in the everydayness of our lives. It is in *lo cotidiano* that we discover what it means to be in relationship with God and others. In the everyday, we learn that faith makes sense when it provides meaning to our experience as women and men whose lives are uniquely shaped by the particularity of our ethnicity and our sociocultural location. *Lo cotidiano* is the school where we hand the faith on to our children, to the new generations of Catholics, and to anyone who is open to perceiving the loving presence of God in the here and now of our daily lives. The complexity of our lived experience continuously invites us to name—and rename—

our reality through expressions, practices, and symbols that point to the sacred. This constitutes what I call our Hispanic Catholic imagination or what theologian Virgilio Elizondo calls "the treasure of Hispanic faith." Such naming indicates that Latinos/as are continuously reading the presence of God in our lives and in our reality with the conviction that we live in a world that is sacred. Lived experience is catechesis at its best because it simultaneously grounds our human experience in the greatness of the Christian revelation while bringing such revelation to fully relate to who we are here and now: human beings created in God's image who search for meaning within the confines of history and whose dignity is inalienable.

Reading Sacred Scripture in *lo cotidiano* is an exercise of transformative dialogue in which we read the text in light of our own experience while allowing the text to read us. Theologian Justo González insightfully articulated such relationship in his book *Santa Biblia: The Bible through Hispanic Eyes* (1996): "To read the Bible is to enter into dialogue with it. In that dialogue, there is a sense in which the text is normative....At the same time, the other pole of the dialogue is just as important. It is I, from my context and perspective, who read the text."

Our lived experience is the context in which we become who we are and witness others "become." Lived experience as a school of catechesis is personal and communal, formative and transformative; it affirms the present and anticipates the future. Consequently, when Latinos/as read Sacred Scripture in this school of catechesis, "we read the Bible, not primarily to find out what we are to do, but to find out who we are and who we are to be," insists González.

POPULAR CATHOLICISM

The experience of God among Latino/a Catholics is deeply shaped by a powerful sense of the sacred perceived in unique ways in the various practices of popular Catholicism. These practices (e.g., *posadas, altarcitos, Viacrucis*) embody an understanding of the faith that is rooted in the particularity of people's lives and experiences. This is the sense in which such practices are to be deemed popular.

Practices of popular Catholicism are articulations rooted in the people's reflection and interpretation of the sources of Christian revelation after significant periods of time—sometimes centuries. Such articulations embody understandings that bring together official convictions and formulations of the faith along with the insights about God, reality, and life of people of faith. Popular Catholicism is simultaneously a way of knowing and perhaps the most available language for the majority of U.S. Latino/a Catholics, many of whom live in the margins of our society, to express our faith in a way that is accessible and familiar.

Popular Catholicism's intrinsic pedagogical character becomes manifest when it serves to hand on the faith of the church, the faith of the people, through practice and symbol. Latinos/as have in popular Catholicism a life-giving resource to learn about the faith of our mothers and fathers, to deepen into the mysteries of that faith, and to transmit what we believe and celebrate to others in the church. Just as the Word of God, available to us in history through Scripture and tradition, is the primary source of catechesis, it is also the primary source of popular Catholicism where it is largely mediated through the experiences of regular women and men living in diverse sociohistorical-cultural contexts. Building on the fact that both catechesis and popular Catholicism share this common source, we can make three observations that have profound pedagogical implications.

First, popular Catholicism and Scripture share a similar matrix: the world of the people. Ecclesial documents on the Scriptures and the work of contemporary biblical scholars coincide with the conviction that the Bible emerged as part of long processes of reflection in various communities, Jewish and Christian. This process took place amid experiences of women and men of faith who did not know that what they wrote or reflected upon would eventually be considered "sacred text." The Jews who wrote the Hebrew Scriptures and the early Christians who articulated the narratives and letters that later became the New Testament had a lot in common with many of the contemporary Christians whose faith is nourished through popular Catholicism: they perceived the world as a sacred place where

God becomes present in incredible ways; they used language (e.g., parables), practices (e.g., annual feasts), and symbols (e.g., Passover) that were part of their everyday lives to speak and interpret their faith; they lived in times where life was constantly defined in terms of struggle. To become familiar with popular Catholicism can be considered as an approximation into the world of the Bible, both in terms of social location as well as in terms of interpretive frameworks.

Second, popular Catholicism teaches us about Sacred Scripture. Nearly all expressions of Latino/a popular Catholicism have a strong biblical background. They are often reenactments of biblical scenes (e.g., *las posadas*, the *Viacrucis*) or are interpretations of biblical themes that become live in particular practices (e.g., *penitentes*). Popular Catholicism serves a catechetical function in the life of the church when it communicates various messages from Sacred Scripture in the form of ritual and symbol. The appeal of popular Catholicism to the senses and to our religious imagination helps us to see biblical moments come to life in the here and now of our experience as a community of faith. The actualization of those biblical moments through popular Catholicism may not be sophisticated enough to suit the critical eye of some theologians and other scholars, or it may seem to be the result of a naive reading, for which there must always be room, of the biblical text, yet it is the people's reading of the sacred text and as such it deserves contemplation. Catechists and teachers who foster participation in practices of popular Catholicism have a great tool that does most of the pedagogical work by itself. The message carried by the practice or the symbol is self-explanatory: it points to a specific element of the treasure of our Christian faith, yet it remains open to other connections and distinct interpretations by the people. Rather than teaching only about Sacred Scripture, popular Catholicism catechizes with Scripture by making the text alive and relevant to people's present experience.

Third, popular Catholicism is renewed by a continuous reading of Sacred Scripture in light of the church's experience here and now. Popular Catholicism should be considered neither as the ultimate interpretation of Sacred Scripture nor the only way to make the biblical message relevant in the life of the people. However, its role in fostering Christian spirituality among Latinos/as must be duly affirmed. Its pedagogical character is enhanced by renewed contact with the sacred text in the liturgy, catechesis, and theological reflection. Women and men involved in catechetical ministry have a responsibility to acquaint people and communities for whom popular Catholicism is a central element in their spiritual lives with the suggested guidelines to read the Bible with the church.

Sacred Scripture and popular Catholicism are intimately related in the various catechetical processes that nurture the life of faith of U.S. Latino/a Catholics. Popular Catholicism is in itself the people's way of "traditioning" their faith; not unrelated or adversarial to official efforts of interpretation of God's Word, yet distinct and complementary: a true expression of the church's *sensus fidelium*.

READING SACRED SCRIPTURE IN SMALL COMMUNITIES

The experience of small ecclesial communities is not foreign to Latino/a Catholics. Reading the Bible, reflecting about faith in the everyday, and celebrating God's Word in small communities has been a hallmark of the Latino/a Catholic experience in Latin America and in the United States. This is how Christianity thrived in its beginnings, flourished in missionary contexts, and continues to be sustained in many parts of the world.

Sacred Scripture has been and remains at the heart of Latino/a small ecclesial communities. Most of these small church cells (also called base communities in some parts of the world) gather around Sacred Scripture to hear the Word of God proclaimed, to pray with it, and to see how the sacred text sheds light into people's particular circumstances. The exercise of reading Sacred Scripture in small communities is powerful and transformative in at least four ways: (1) it empowers us to access Sacred Scripture as a text that speaks to us in the here and now of their everyday; (2) it introduces us to a transformative dialogue with God's Word in the Bible that invites to conversion; (3) it fosters a deeper understanding of God's divine revelation; and (4) it creates communion among those who read the text together within the church. This experience is pedagogical in nature and, consequently, every catechetical effort among Latinos/as should look at small ecclesial communities as privileged spaces to hand on the faith of the church.

Church statements make reference to the great value of small ecclesial communities in the evangelization of Latinos/as. *Encuentro and Mission: A Renewed Pastoral Framework for Hispanic Ministry* (2002), a pastoral statement by the U.S. bishops refocusing the church's commitment to Hispanic ministry in the country, looks favorably to small ecclesial communities. The statement affirms that these communities "have been and continue to be a valuable expression of the evangelization efforts of the church" (no. 41); they are effective for promoting leadership formation. Citing an earlier document also written by the U.S. Catholic bishops, *Communion and Mission: A Guide for Bishops and Pastoral Leaders on Small Church Communities*, on the value of these communities, *Encuentro and Mission* corroborates that when "solidly rooted in Scripture, church tradition, and Hispanic religiosity, small church communities constitute a new moment in the church's self-understanding, epitomizing the celebration and proclamation of the church" (see *Encuentro and Mission* 25). In 2007, the bishops of Latin America and the Caribbean met in Aparecida, Brazil, for their Fifth General Conference. Some bishops and leaders from the United States participated in the gathering. Their presence was very significant considering that millions of Latino/a Catholics now living in the United States were formed within the structures of the church in Latin America and bring that experience as a part of our gift to the church in the United States. Aparecida speaks of small communities as "schools that have helped form Christians committed to their faith, disciples and missionaries of the Lord" (no. 178). These communities are instrumental to "enable the people to have access to greater knowledge of the Word of God, social commitment in the name of the gospel, the emergence of new lay services, and education of the faith of adults" (no. 178).

Indeed, these are not the only everyday moments of encounter with the sacred where catechesis and Word of God meet as part of the experience of U.S. Latino/a Catholics. The goal of this reflection has been to assert that there are unique moments within the Latino/a Catholic experience that have a significant catechetical value and that these must be seen as privileged opportunities to foster a forming and transforming encounter with God's Word. For catechists working with Latino/a Catholics, these are great resources to advance the ministry of sharing faith.

11

Hispanics and Family Life

Hosffman Ospino

The Catholic experience in the United States in the twenty-first century is in the midst of a major transformation. To be more exact,
it is in the midst of a major cultural, demographic, and socioreligious transformation. At the heart of such phenomenon is the fast-
growing Hispanic presence: more than 40 percent of all Catholics in
the country self-identify as Hispanic. As Catholics in this country, we
cannot speak of family life these days without paying attention to
what it means to be a Hispanic family and the major dynamics that
shape the experience of this population.

What do we need to do as pastoral leaders, counselors, and
scholars to best accompany Catholic families today in the United
States? This is a very important question, mindful that the health
of our church, as a community of faith, and that of the larger society often reflect the health of family life. The more we invest in the
family, especially addressing the dynamics associated with raising
the next generation of Catholics, and the support of couples to live
stable relationships so they can raise healthy children, the stronger
we will be as church and society.

The accompaniment of the Hispanic family does not happen in a vacuum. I propose that we look closely at how Catholic parishes can do this. The parish is the space where many pastoral efforts of outreach to Hispanic families have a chance to flourish. Parishes are privileged spaces where Hispanic families interested in celebrating what they believe, passing on the faith to the younger generations, and growing in their relationship with Jesus Christ coincide. Granted, millions of Hispanic Catholics are not involved in parish life on a regular basis. Millions are "nominal Catholics" who come to parishes sporadically, often to receive a sacrament or to participate in a ritual (e.g., a funeral, a wedding, a baptism). Nevertheless, it is in the context of the parish where most of the formal pastoral outreach to Hispanic Catholic families takes place.

The parish continues to be the center of spiritual and pastoral life for most practicing Catholics in the United States, immigrant and U.S.-born. The first point of contact for Catholic immigrants with the church in the country is usually a parish. Even though more than 4,000 Catholic parishes have closed during the last five decades, the network of more than 16,900 Catholic parishes in the United States remains one of the largest and strongest in the world. U.S. Catholics frequently speak of Hispanic parishes. There are approximately 4,500 parishes with Hispanic ministry or about 25 percent of all Catholic parishes in the United States. These are not the "national parishes" of the past, communities built by national groups to meet their own spiritual and pastoral needs isolated from other parochial and national communities. They are regular territorial communities serving large bodies of Hispanic Catholics, mostly immigrants and their children and grandchildren.

I propose that ministries aiming at supporting Hispanic Catholic families in the context of the parish focus on the following three priorities:

1. EMPHASIS ON YOUNG ADULT FAMILIES

There is no doubt that an approach to supporting family life in the Hispanic Catholic community must begin with serious attention to the young. Hispanic ministry is de facto young adult ministry and youth ministry. Many Catholic family ministries in our country focus on engaging grandparents and supporting families where the parents are in their midlife years. This often means helping adult Catholics to renew marital commitments, support them as they make financial decisions that will affect their retirement years, and deal with the transitions that come when children leave home for college or professional life. There is a growing number of ministries focused on supporting the spiritual growth of couples (e.g., retreats, support groups), many of which require some level of socioeconomic stability and have somehow settled into a geographical region where such resources exist.

While all these are important, most Hispanics in the United States are far from those ages and from the socioeconomic stability that many of such ministries presuppose. We are confronted with a very young population for whom family life means being a U.S.-born child or adolescent, often being raised by an immigrant parent—or being exposed to the influence of an immigrant adult at home. For many Hispanic Catholics, family life begins with the rocky dynamics of having children in the late teens and early twenties, too often out of wedlock. Socioeconomic stability for many of these young couples is rather a dream that few will ever achieve, considering the low levels of educational attainment among Hispanics (e.g., only 16 percent of Hispanic adults have a four-year college degree) and the lack of access to good education for most (e.g., more than 70 percent of school-age Hispanic children attend underperforming public schools; only 4 percent of school-age Catholic children attend Catholic schools).

Considering how young Hispanics are, family ministries with this population must focus on the young adult population. This means that such ministries are to begin with assisting such families, and those who are about to start family life, to gain some form of social, economic, emotional, and religious stability. Ministry with this particular population places pastoral leaders before the situation of working with young people raising young people. Family ministries in the Hispanic community, therefore, must be planned in close conversation with catechetical initiatives and youth ministry programs. Finally, because the vast majority of Hispanics under the age of thirty are born and raised in the United States, family ministries with this population cannot be limited to replicating models of ministry used primarily with immigrants or models imported from Spanish-speaking countries. We need models of family ministry that respond to the needs and expectations of a population highly influenced in its values and societal upbringing by the larger U.S. culture, especially in urban settings where most Hispanics live, while retaining socioreligious and cultural elements of an immigrant generation that still exerts major influence upon them. Of course, doing this under the current models of Hispanic ministry, which focus primarily and sometimes exclusively upon the immigrant population, represents a major challenge.

2. ADVOCACY AND ACCOMPANIMENT

Family ministries that aim at serving Hispanic Catholics require an intentional understanding of the socioeconomic realities affecting this population. Pastoral leaders working with Hispanic families cannot pretend to bring the best of our Catholic spiritual resources about family life while ignoring the complex everyday realities that shape the lives of these couples and their children. The fact that about 23 percent of Hispanics live in deep poverty and another 50 percent are slightly above the poverty level should give us pause as pastoral leaders. Hispanic families are profoundly impacted by dynamics such as domestic violence, high levels of incarceration (Hispanics constitute the second largest prison population in the United States), undocumented immigration, and the effects of family separation because of deportations. Because of the low levels of educational attainment affecting most Hispanics, mobility into the middle class is a very slow process. Millions of Hispanic adults work in the agricultural and service industries, which are known for paying low wages.

These circumstances, among many others, make a vision of Catholic family ministry that promotes homeschooling, regular engagement in retreats, counseling sessions that require high-levels of sophistication, and even the idea of a parent to stay home full time to care for young children practically unattainable for millions of Hispanic Catholics. This does not mean that pastoral leaders in parishes and elsewhere are to give up on such practices. They should remain as cherished possibilities, yet we need pastoral approaches to family ministry that start where Hispanics are, in the contexts where they live, and address the socioeconomic realities that shape their lives. We need models of family ministry that build upon patient, caring, and merciful accompaniment:

> An evangelizing community gets involved by word and deed in people's daily lives; it bridges distances, it is willing to abase itself if necessary, and it embraces human life, touching the suffering flesh of Christ in others. Evangelizers thus take on the "smell of the sheep" and the sheep are willing to hear their voice....Evangelization consists mostly of patience and disregard for constraints of time. (*Evangelii Gaudium* 24)

Catholic pastoral outreach to Hispanic families in the context of the parish demands a strong element of advocacy. If we want Hispanic Catholics to form strong families, then we need to advocate as a community of faith for conditions where such families can thrive. Let me mention at least five areas of advocacy that can be part of our Catholic family ministries: better wages and treatment of farmworkers (the majority are Hispanic), immigration policies that privilege family reunification, better education of Hispanic children and youth in public educational institutions, access to quality healthcare, and better support systems that lead to the reduction of poverty. Without improvement of these social dynamics, one cannot credibly expect that Hispanic Catholics can form stable and thriving families.

3. ADULT FAITH FORMATION THAT LEADS TO A STRONGER UNDERSTANDING OF FAMILY LIFE

At the heart of strong family ministries must be a strong catechesis that leads Catholics to understand well, embrace, and live the vision for the family that the church communicates as part of its evangelizing mission. Catholic pastoral leaders may sometimes take for granted that because someone is baptized as a Catholic or belongs to a cultural tradition with strong Catholic roots, therefore there is a clear understanding of the church's vision about family life. If that is the case, the assumption is naive. While most Hispanics self-identify as Catholic, particularly the majority of the twenty million Hispanic immigrants living in the country, many struggle to understand the church's vision about family life and marriage, and it is likely that many have never heard it articulated because of lack of appropriate faith formation. Studies on religious literacy often reveal that Hispanic Catholics have a strong sense of family life and a profound spirituality, yet at the time of naming or articulating their faith, they struggle. While one may "get by" with some form of cultural Catholicism in a Latin American society where most of the population is Catholic, such is not always the case in the United States. The proof of this is the low number of sacramental marriages among Hispanic Catholics nationwide, the lack of family participation in Sunday Mass, and the struggle of many Hispanic adults to pass on the faith to their young, especially those born in the United States.

Parishes with Hispanic ministry should be the ideal place for Hispanics—especially for immigrants, since most Hispanic parish ministry happens in Spanish—to access adult faith formation about family life and marriage. Yet this is not happening in most of these parishes. Where it happens, on average the numbers are very small: less than twenty persons enrolled in adult faith formation programs, according to the 2014 National Study of Catholic Parishes with Hispanic Ministry. This is why a good pastoral strategy for family ministry among Hispanic Catholics should be the strengthening of adult faith formation programs and initiatives with this particular focus.

However, faith formation about family life should not wait until adult life. It is imperative that all Catholic programs of faith formation, starting with those engaging the youngest children, have strong components and units about family life. Every Catholic should reach adulthood with a clear understanding and appreciation of the church's vision about family life.

The vibrancy of Catholic family life in the United States in the rest of this century will be closely linked to how Hispanic Catholics form, cultivate, and support families. We have a major task on our hands engaging this population, especially young Hispanics. To do so, we must embrace a language that challenges the so-called two churches paradigm. That is, language that speaks of Hispanic Catholics as if we were visitors or outliers, assuming that there is an established church—mostly white, Euro-American, middle-class, and English-speaking—that out of benevolence "welcomes" or "serves" a body of Catholics that look, speak, and celebrate their faith in different ways. There is only one Catholic Church in the United States and Hispanics, as well as Catholics from various cultural communities, are an integral part of it. If we care about Catholic family life, we must first see ourselves as one church.

I conclude this reflection with a call to action: Let's support Catholic family life in the United States by making a preferential option for young and young adult Hispanic Catholics, advocating and accompanying them as they form the families that are the backbone of our Catholic faith communities, and offering them the best faith formation resources so they can grow in the church's vision for family life.

12

Young Hispanic Catholics

Hosffman Ospino

About 60 percent of all Catholics younger than eighteen and nearly half (46 percent) of all Catholic millennials (ages eighteen to thirty-four) in the United States are Hispanic. The numbers speak loudly and clearly. We no longer need to imagine a future when Hispanics become a numerical majority among U.S. Catholics. That future is already here. In many corners of the United States and in thousands of faith communities, to speak of Catholicism is to speak of how Hispanic Catholics live and celebrate their relationship with Jesus Christ.

Two simple yes-or-no questions for the reader: Are you and your parish/organization genuinely engaging young Hispanic Catholics? Have you taken the appropriate time to understand the experience of this important population? The answers should determine a path of action, with the following observations serving as a roadmap. How well we engage young Hispanic Catholics *now* will significantly define the vibrancy of U.S. Catholicism for the rest of this century.

HISPANIC AND (STILL) CATHOLIC

Although Hispanics have been present in the U.S. territory for more than five hundred years, during the last half century the Hispanic presence has experienced an accelerated growth, literally doubling every ten years. Migration waves from Latin America and the Spanish-speaking Caribbean have played a major role. About twenty million Hispanic immigrants live in the country today; about two-thirds self-identify as Catholic. Nevertheless, it is the children and grandchildren of these immigrants who are driving much of the demographic change in the Catholic Church. Two-thirds of Hispanics are U.S. born. Catholic self-identification is not as strong in this group as in the case of the immigrant generation, yet most young Hispanics still see themselves as Catholic.

Hispanics are in general a very young population. The average age is twenty-nine. About 58 percent of Hispanics are younger than thirty-three. We know that nine out of ten Hispanics younger than eighteen (94 percent) and about half of Hispanic millennials were born in the United States. Most of these young women and men have embraced many core aspects of the predominant culture in which they live. They speak English as their everyday language, their lives are shaped by the regular use of technology and social media, and they find themselves constantly negotiating the influence of multiple cultural trends like their peers. They are American young people in the full sense of the phrase.

At the same time, most young Latinos/as remain culturally Hispanic. This means that they continue to be nurtured by values and practices from the various Hispanic/Latino cultures that coexist in neighborhoods, towns, and cities throughout the United States. The Hispanic cultural and religious influence is channeled in various ways, most importantly through the family. Many young Hispanics presently live in households with at least one immigrant parent or relative. Pastoral experience indicates that immigrants tend to be more intentional in the process of fostering a sense of religious identity among the younger generations, usually drawing from what they learned in their countries of origin.

Young Latinos/as participate in a strong Catholic imagination that pervades much of Hispanic cultures. Young Hispanics are more likely than other young Catholics to participate in Marian devotions and other practices of popular Catholicism. One cannot minimize the importance of the *quinceañera* ritual—with its mixture of religious and secular elements—among many young Hispanics and their families. The use of iconic representations of Jesus and Mary is common within this group. Young adult Hispanic Catholic couples often baptize their children and bring them for first communion and confirmation, even though most are not sacramentally married nor are actively involved in parish life.

FLUID IDENTITIES, CHALLENGING PARADIGMS

Pastoral leaders and educators working with young Hispanic Catholics need to remain aware of the various factors that make the experience of this group particularly complex. Not only must they journey along the normal process of becoming adults and negotiating the challenges of growing up in the U.S. sociocultural context, but they must also sort out who they are as Hispanics in the United States.

In the early 2000s, Instituto Fe y Vida, a national Catholic Hispanic organization focused on youth and young adults, acknowledged that there is not one all-encompassing category that fully captures the experience of young Hispanics. Instituto leaders proposed four pastoral categories to name the fluid reality of Latino/a adolescents: identity seekers, mainstream movers, immigrant workers, and gang members and high-risk teens. These categories remain helpful and easily correlate to the experience of Hispanic young adults. From a religious perspective and considering their growing numbers, I would add a fifth category: Hispanic "nones" (i.e., nonreligiously affiliated), with particular attention to former Catholics. There is much to learn from this group to assess present pastoral initiatives and envision new ones.

Young Hispanic Catholics are most likely bilingual and bicultural. These young women and men are both Hispanic and American. They are Catholic like their immigrant relatives and religious like other young Christians in the country who are figuring out how to incorporate their faith into their lives amidst pluralism. When contending with these binaries, adults and pastoral leaders are often tempted to expect that young Hispanics must choose one or the other. Such expectation reflects an either/or mentality that often prevails at home, at church, and in the larger society.

In various ministerial contexts, immigrant adults typically want U.S.-born, young Hispanics to remain culturally and religiously like them. In turn, Catholics of different backgrounds often expect that these young women and men embrace models of ministry that have worked well primarily with Euro-American young Catholics, as if such models were culturally neutral and always adaptable. Another common expectation is that young Hispanics become fully "Americanized," hinting at the idea that to do this they must abandon the language and cultural roots of their relatives. All such expectations are rather unrealistic and impractical. Pushing them too much can have negative consequences. Let us not forget that youth ministry initiatives normally reflect the vision of reality that we hold as well as our understanding of young people.

Catholic parishes and dioceses nationwide continue to discern best approaches to meet the spiritual and pastoral needs of Hispanic youth. Communities that bank on the idea that young Hispanics should learn and practice their faith more like their immigrant relatives tend to invest in initiatives that are mostly in Spanish and replicate models that were developed somewhere else, yet may not have the same effectiveness within the U.S. socioreligious context. Communities that overly rely on assimilationist perspectives get caught up in a vicious cycle of ignoring or dismissing the potential of what young Hispanics bring in terms of faith and culture, while imposing models that may not necessarily respond to the needs of communities that are culturally diverse, multilingual, and not always middle or upper class.

The main consequence of this prevalent either/or mentality is the marginalization of this important group of Catholics, upon whom much of the future of U.S. Catholicism depends. Marginalization in turn leads to isolation, and ultimately to defection. It is painful, yet not surprising, that in recent decades about fourteen million Hispanics in the United States (one in four) stopped self-identifying as Catholic, most of them young and born in the United States. They drifted away. These are not necessarily disaffected young Catholics or people inclined to reject religion altogether. In fact, one can confidently assert that, given their rootedness in the vibrant Hispanic cultures from which they draw inspiration, religion still plays an important role in their lives.

In the not-so-distant past, Catholic schools and colleges played a major role in supporting Catholic youth. These spaces proved to be very effective, preparing millions of young Catholics to succeed in society and to grow in their faith. Hundreds of thousands of young women and men from Catholic educational institutions went on to exercise important leadership roles in the church (e.g., priests, vowed religious, and lay ecclesial ministers) and the larger society. Nevertheless, now that Hispanics are the majority of young Catholics, very few benefit from such institutions. As of 2021 only 4 percent of school-age Hispanic Catholic children are enrolled in Catholic schools (about 320,000 of 8 million), and a mere 13.7 percent of students enrolled in Catholic colleges (approx. 123,000) are Hispanic.

While there are many signs of hope, overall, the challenges for passing on the faith to young Latinos are immense. A worrisome combination of prejudice, unrealistic expectations, and lack of investment in intentional pastoral accompaniment is imperiling how young Hispanic Catholics discern their vocations as Christian disciples here and now as well as their commitment to faith communities that often fall short of understanding and affirming their potential.

SEIZE THE MOMENT

My hope is that this brief analysis serves as a wake-up call and a motivation for Catholic pastoral leaders and organizations to redouble our outreach efforts toward this population. We must seize the moment! Seizing the moment demands making major commitments. I would like to suggest three. First, we must ensure that young Hispanics see the church as a home where they belong. Parishes and schools in particular need to make a preferential option for pastoral initiatives that sincerely welcome and engage these young Catholics. Second, we must create spaces where young Hispanics encounter Jesus Christ in truly transforming ways and nurture their Christian vocation. This is a time for faith formation initiatives that are creative and take culture, language, and social location seriously. Third, we must accompany young Hispanic Catholics in the contexts and realities in which their lives unfold. Millions of them live on the peripheries of church and society. Ministry to young Hispanic Catholics in the United States must be defined by its prophetic character.

Young Hispanics are a blessing to the Catholic Church in the United States. It is time to embrace this blessing.